T0326608

Economic Assistance and the Northern Ireland Conflict

Economic Assistance and the Northern Ireland Conflict

Building the Peace Dividend

Sean Byrne

Madison · Teaneck
Fairleigh Dickinson University Press

© 2009 by Rosemont Publishing and Printing Corp.

All rights reserved. Authorization to photocopy items for internal or personal use, or the internal or personal use of specific clients, is granted by the copyright owner, provided that a base fee of $10.00, plus eight cents per page, per copy is paid directly to the Copyright Clearance Center, 222 Rosewood Drive, Danvers, Massachusetts 01923. [978-0-8386-4186-6/09 $10.00 + 8¢ pp, pc.]

Associated University Presses
2010 Eastpark Boulevard
Cranbury, NJ 08512

The paper used in this publication meets the requirements of the American National Standard for Permanence of Paper for Printed Library Materials Z39.48-1984.

Library of Congress Cataloging-in-Publication Data
Byrne, Sean, 1962-
    Economic assistance and the Northern Ireland conflict : building the peace dividend / Sean Byrne.
        p. cm.—
    Includes bibliographical references and index.
    ISBN 978-0-8386-4186-6
    1. Economic assistance—Northern Ireland.   2. Peace-building—Northern Ireland.   3. Political violence—Northern Ireland.   4. Northern Ireland—Politics and government—20th century.   5. Conflict management—Northern Ireland.   I Title.
    HC257.N58B97 2009
    338.9109416--dc22   2008021107

PRINTED IN THE UNITED STATES OF AMERICA

Dedication

This book is dedicated to my aunts, Kathleen Reilly and Anna-Rose McGurn (née Reilly), Enniskillen, Co. Fermanagh, who passed away in 1998 and 2003, respectively. Anna-Rose and Kate taught me many valuable lessons about life. Their basic respect and love for people transcended distinctions of politics, nationality, creed, wealth, and social standing. I miss them both dearly. I remember my late father-in-law, David Senehi, a person of wisdom, peace, and integrity, and the late Tom Conlan, O'Brien's Bridge, Co. Clare, poet, scholar, and seanachai. Also, I honor the memory of Professor Stephen Koff, my friend and mentor in the Department of Political Science, Maxwell School of Citizenship and Public Affairs, Syracuse University, who passed away in 2005, and who had a profound influence on my intellectual development.

Contents

Preface and Acknowledgments

THERE IS NO BOOK ON ECONOMIC ASSISTANCE and peace building in Northern Ireland quite like this one—a study that focuses on the key role of economic aid in building the peace in protracted ethnopolitical conflict after the violence has ended. I recognize the need for a book that makes the role of economic aid in postconflict societies interesting and relevant to students, policy makers, funding agencies, nongovernmental organizations, civil servants, and conflict resolution practitioners, having taken both undergraduate and graduate courses on the politics of Northern Ireland with Professor John Coakley and Professor Brigid Laffan, College of Humanities, University of Limerick; courses on ethnic conflicts with Professors Paul Bew, Adrian Guelke, and Frank Wright, Department of Politics, Queen's University of Belfast; and Professor Stephen Koff, Department of Political Science, Maxwell School of Citizenship and Public Affairs, Syracuse University.

This book presents economic assistance in Northern Ireland in the context of analysis, intervention, prevention, and policy making. Significant emphasis is placed on the perceptions of civil servants, funding agency development officers, and community leaders funded by one or both external funding agencies, the International Fund for Ireland (IFI) and the European Union (EU) Peace and Reconciliation Program or Peace I Fund. A central theme of the book is the value of targeted economic assistance by external funding agencies in building the peace dividend in Northern Ireland.

The research is based on the qualitative analysis of thirty-five in-depth and open-ended interviews with Belfast and Dublin civil servants, IFI and EU Peace I funding agency development officers, and community leaders of funded projects. Findings demonstrate, in general, that the respondents welcome targeted economic assistance, perceiving that it is critical to economic development and the empowerment of marginalized communities in the postconflict peace building process under way in Northern Ireland. The respondents report that the central bureaucracies in Belfast and Dublin are not in tune with the needs of local communities and their proposed projects. In addition, they suggest that the application process must be streamlined, and that more funding agency development officers should be put on the ground to work with the Protestant Unionist and Catholic Nationalist communities. Funding agency development

9

officers and community leaders generally feel that economic assistance is facilitating "single-identity" rather than cross-community reconciliation work. The participants also believe that by taking steps to resolve the conflict, a political solution must be taken into consideration in addition to providing economic assistance.

The study suggests, based on these findings, that funding agencies must design and develop a comprehensive action and community partnership model and strategic plans to meet complex urban and rural community needs. Bridging a gap between understanding the micro-macro socioeconomic causes of the Northern Ireland conflict within the strategic role of external economic aid in building the peace dividend, this approach provides the nexus between theory, practice, policy making, and conflict transformation. I conclude with key insights derived from the Northern Ireland study for policy makers using targeted economic assistance in a process of integrated peace-building strategies to address the deep structural roots of socioeconomic conflict in other postconflict societies.

I also wish to thank Dr. Arthur V. Mauro, OC, OM, QC, KSG, who has made it possible for me to work at such a wonderful and important center as a result of his generous gifts and farsightedness. I want to thank Pam Mason for copyediting the manuscript and Jobb Arnold, Marcie Hawranik, Gayle Roncin, Katerina Standish, and Pauline Tennent, research assistants in the Arthur V. Mauro Centre of Peace and Justice, for proofreading the manuscript and for assisting me in compiling the bibliography. I wish to thank Niall Byrne, Jennifer Ruiz-Byrne, Jessica Senehi, Alan Conlan, Eyob Fissuh, Mislav Matic, Amos Nadan, Dan Lenoski, Cynthia Irvin, Marie Olson-Lounsbery, Fred Pearson, Tom Boudreau, Dennis Sandole, Chris Cunningham, John Stapleton, David Creamer, and John Perry for reading various drafts of this book. I thank my parents, Michael and Patricia Byrne, for the many hours and days they spent with me during the summer of 1997 driving around the border towns to all of my interview appointments, and for discussing local history and politics with me in a profound and stimulating way. I am forever grateful for the love and dedication of my wife, Dr. Jessica Senehi, my sister, Jennifer, and brother, Niall. My six-year-old precocious daughter, Katie Byrne, has a big heart and a beautiful smile for such a wee wane; she gives me inspiration for the future. Finally, I thank the Mauro Center, St. Paul's College for giving me a small research grant in 2004 as well as the Social Science and Humanities Research Council of Canada and the United States Institute of Peace for making this study and my book possible by providing research grants in 2005 and 1996 to Dr. Cynthia Irvin and myself.

Abbreviations

ADM	Area Development Management
AIA	Anglo-Irish Agreement
ANC	African National Congress
ASUs	Active Service Units
BBC	British Broadcasting Corporation
CLMC	Combined Loyalist Military Command
CRC	Community Relations Council
CRISP	Community Regeneration Improvement Special Program
DANI	Department of Agriculture for Northern Ireland
DENI	Department of Education in the North
DFP	Department of Finance and Personnel
DOE	Department of the Environment
DUP	Democratic Unionist Party
ECU	European currency units
EU	European Union
GAA	Gaelic Athletic Association
GFA	Good Friday Agreement
GGA	Global Grants Agreement
IFBs	Intermediary Funding Bodies
IFI	International Fund for Ireland
IMF	International Monetary Fund
INGOs	international nongovernmental organizations
IRA	Irish Republican Army
MEPs	Members of the European Parliament
MNCs	multinational corporations
NGOs	nongovernmental organizations
NI	Northern Ireland
NICDA	Northern Ireland Co-operative Development Agency
NICRA	Northern Ireland Civil Rights Association
NIVT	Northern Ireland Voluntary Trust
NORAID	Northern Aid
OECD	Organization of Economic Co-operation and Development
OUP	Official Unionist Party
PA	Palestinian Authority
PIRA	Provisional Irish Republican Army
PM	prime minister

RIRA	Real Irish Republican Army
RTÉ	Radio Telifís Éireann
RUC	Royal Ulster Constabulary
SADF	South African Defense Force
SAS	Special Airborne Service
SDLP	Social Democratic and Labour Party
SF	Sinn Féin
TCR	transformational conflict resolution
UDA	Ulster Defense Association
UDR	Ulster Defense Regiment
UVF	Ulster Volunteer Force

Economic Assistance and the Northern Ireland Conflict

1

The International Fund for Ireland and the European Union Peace I Fund: Building the Peace Dividend in Northern Ireland

INTRODUCTION

THIS STUDY EVALUATES THE PROCESS, GOALS, and outcome of external economic assistance in building the peace dividend in Northern Ireland (NI), as well as the perceptions of the politics and practice of its delivery and distribution, and the effects, if any, that international assistance has had on the dynamics of both inter- and intraethnic conflict and cooperation. It represents one of the first comprehensive analyses of people's perceptions of the initial phase of an ongoing historical process that involves the International Fund for Ireland (IFI), established by Britain and the Republic of Ireland in 1986, and the European Union's (EUs) Special Support Program for Peace and Reconciliation in Ireland, or Peace I (1995–99), begun in 1994 to help lay the foundations for a sustainable and durable peace. The Peace II phase (2000–2006) has just ended, and the final phase of the funding process, Peace III, is under way (2007–13). Perceptions were identified and qualitatively analyzed from original data gathered during the summer of 1997 using semistructured interviews with some thirty-five community leaders, development officers, and civil servants on both sides of the NI/Irish Republic border.

This study also addresses the related propositions (frequently asserted, but seldom empirically demonstrated) that economic growth mitigates interethnic conflict, and that external economic assistance can nurture interethnic reconciliation and facilitate the resolution of protracted ethnic conflicts. Most studies of international peace-building assistance programs have focused on issues of delivery, distribution, and product. This project seeks to remedy, in part, the lack of empirical data on the complex relationship between economic assistance and ethnic conflict by going beyond previous studies of economic policy in NI (O'Dowd, Rolston, and Tomlinsion 1980; Rolston and Tomlinson 1988; Rowthorn and Wayne 1988; Teague 1987; Tomlinson 1995), which have been confined to single-case examinations of specific initiatives and their effect on the Protestant and Catholic communities.

The perception that economic prosperity, interethnic cooperation, and conflict transformation are interrelated can be seen in a number of recent political and economic initiatives. These seek, or have sought, to facilitate conflict settlements and the consolidation of democracy in the Middle East, South Africa, Sri Lanka, the countries of the former Yugoslavia, El Salvador, and NI. Of these, however, NI is one of the few cases to offer a long historical record of economic and political initiatives aimed at reducing, if not always resolving, the continuing conflict. Examples of these are the 1983 New Ireland Forum, the 1984 MacBride Principles, the 1995 Joint Framework for Agreement Document, and the 1998 Good Friday Agreement (GFA). All of these will be examined later in the chapter.

In 1995, U.S. president Bill Clinton committed a triangulated partnership between the U.S. government, the British and Irish governments, and the business community to "provide jobs and economic stability to support the peace process" (White House Conference 1995, 2). Similarly, the European Union Commission took into account the necessity of promoting NI's economic and social development, explicitly acknowledging that "the EU has a clear interest and vital role to play in maintaining the momentum for peace by means of a special support program for NI and the Border counties" (European Union Structural Funds 1999, 11). The NI conflict, therefore, is an excellent choice for a "theory-building" case study of the effects of economic growth/decline on levels of violence, interethnic attitudes (cooperative/hostile), and conflict reduction (Esman 1991). Moreover, this work extends and complements earlier studies of the role of external economic assistance toward building the peace process in NI.

By relating attitudes toward the role of external economic aid in building peace in NI, the work extends Anderson (1999), Berdal and Malone (2000), Boyce (2000, 2005), Brynen (2000, 2005), Cousens, Kumar, and Wermester (2000), Escobar (1994), Esman (1991, 1994, 1995, 1997), Forman and Patrick (2000), Jeong (2005), Lederach (1997), Pugh and Goodhand (2005), Wenger and Mockli (2005), and Woodward's work (2005) on the role of economic aid in protracted ethnic conflicts. It complements Bew et al. (1995) and Cunningham's (1991, 1994) work on the connection between economic deprivation and conflict in NI and builds on the work of Esman (1991, 1995, 1997) and Lederach (1997) by exploring how recipients of international postconflict peace-building aid perceive the politics and the possibilities of that aid in promoting and sustaining postconflict reconciliation and reconstruction.

In a study of this kind, it is important to generate diagnoses so that conflict resolution practitioners and policy makers might develop prescriptions in partnership with both parties in the conflict. It is critical to observe what worked or did not work, and what other factors have influenced the success of a program so that policy makers can use economic aid to build the peace dividend in other postconflict societies too.

This research maps people's political images of the role of economic assistance in sustainable economic development, community empowerment, reconciliation, and in building the peace dividend in NI. Specifically, different patterns of political imagery indicate important dimensions of the role of economic assistance in peace building and the transformation of the NI conflict. By expanding these respondents' political imagery, this project also significantly expands existing work on economic aid and peace building in Bosnia, Cyprus, Guatemala, Nicaragua, and the Palestinian Authority. The current changing political and socioeconomic context within NI reflects that a process of peace building has begun and that external economic assistance is a cornerstone of that process. Even though political and, to a lesser extent, economic circumstances have changed considerably in NI in subsequent years, and since economic conditions in the Irish Republic have improved dramatically in the last decade, it is most important to study the role of external economic assistance in building the peace dividend, as this systematic analysis of the qualitative data sheds new light on the impact of economic assistance in the postconflict peace building process.

This book contributes methodologically to the analysis and resolution of protracted ethnopolitical conflicts as well as generating knowledge concerning the effects of external economic aid in building capacity and reconciliation in postconflict societies. Its findings provide a sound base for further comparative research on the role of economic assistance in building the peace dividend in ethnopolitical conflicts.

METHODOLOGY, DATA, AND ANALYTICAL PROCEDURES

This project documents the empirical relationship between the level of conflict in NI, the development of economic policy and offers of external economic assistance, and conflict settlement initiatives. It traces the delivery of the promised assistance, analyzing the patterns of its distribution. Public attitudes regarding the efficacy of economic development in facilitating interethnic cooperation and conflict resolution are empirically assessed through interviews with community leaders and development officers, and IFI and EU Peace I grantees. The project concludes with an attempt to identify those approaches that most effectively promote both economic development and interethnic reconciliation. In the long term, the specific objective of this work is to develop a computerized database of data on the NI economy and economic policy, interview transcripts, and opinion surveys, which can be used to assess both quantitatively and qualitatively the effects of external economic assistance on the peace process in NI. I also plan to do a follow-up study in NI as well as to extend the research agenda to other ethnopolitical conflicts.

RESEARCH DESIGN

This study made use of a distinct methodology, yielding rich qualitative interpretations and comparisons to explore the relationships claimed previously between economic growth (decline), levels of violence, interethnic cooperation/hostility, and conflict reduction initiatives. To document the evolution and changes of economic policy, development, and external economic assistance in NI since 1969, I first made use of the extensive collection of materials related to the conflict from appropriate documents available from government and EU bureaus located in Dublin and Belfast. Case studies were drawn from organizations funded either by the IFI and/or the EU Peace I Fund. The first set was primarily concerned with issues related to interethnic conciliation and cooperation while organizations in the second set focused primarily on community economic development in NI and the border region.

The spillover of the conflict has devastated the economic infrastructure of towns and villages that dot the border area. People living in rural areas have experienced the NI conflict in a different way than urbanites. Hence, Harris (1972) and Whyte (1990) report a rural-urban split in NI, and suggest that social science researchers must take this factor into account in the research design and fieldwork stage of research projects.

In addition to regional differences (rural/urban), the respondents are different from each other by virtue of class, gender, religion, spatial milieu, and experience of the political conflict. The community group leaders are both Nationalist and Unionist and are a random representative sample of the funded community projects of their areas. External economic aid from both funds targets the areas of greatest social need, particularly within the Nationalist community, which has borne the brunt of poverty and deprivation in the past. The Nationalist perspective is critically important, especially regarding the role of economic aid in providing Nationalists with human and material resources to build self-confidence and self-esteem that promotes an atmosphere of politics rather than political violence (Byrne and Irvin 2001, 2002).

Taking all of that into consideration, an interview instrument was developed, field-tested, and administered to a representative sample of NI's population in Derry, Dublin, and the border area. The preparation and organization of the field research stage was devised carefully. Formal letters were sent in March 1997 to community groups, civil servants, and agency development consultants outlining my research interest.

Most people responded positively to follow-up phone calls requesting an interview for when I would arrive that summer. These were set up well in advance, and as contacts were made with individuals, other interviews followed.

The research addresses three empirical questions: (1) What roles do the IFI and the EU Peace I agencies play in the distribution of economic resources? (2) What do community groups feel about the funding processes generally? and, (3) Does external economic aid promote economic development and peace and reconciliation? These questions explore participants' assumptions about the impact of both funding agencies on economic development, and whether community economic development can constructively impact the NI conflict.

The format was based on face-to-face interviews, typically held in the individual's workplace. However, for security reasons they sometimes took place at a pub. My knowledge and experience of NI allowed me to understand cultural nuances and to connect easily with each of the respondents. I made sure that I arrived on time and began each interview, building rapport and putting each person at his or her ease. All of the interviewees were told that they were being interviewed as part of a research project on economic development and the NI conflict. While complete anonymity was guaranteed to every person, the majority of people said that it was not a problem to use their names. I assured those participants who requested anonymity that fictitious names would be used in any published research. I do not refer to any names in this study. Moreover, respondents were asked if they fully understood the nature of the research project before we commenced. The interviewing process went very smoothly and the cooperation received from everyone was remarkable.

The Interview Process

The analysis aims to generate a greater interpretive understanding of the meanings individuals engaged in or affected by community economic development organizations attach to their experiences of these projects. The choice of a theoretical framework, research questions, interview guide, research sites, and research participants was an essential aspect of the data analysis (Druckman 2005).

Many sources identify three major categories of interviewing structures: the standardized or formal interview, the unstructured or informal interview, and the semistructured or guided interview (Druckman 2005; Denzin 1989). Druckman identifies two ways of doing in-depth interviewing: unstructured and semistructured or focused interviewing. Semistructured interviews provide the investigator with a deep assortment of information, allowing deeper insights into the respondents' ideas and meanings (Bogdan and Biklin 1992; Druckman 2005). Participants can then easily express their thoughts about the subject matter at hand (Peshkin 1993). As mentioned earlier, the particular method of in-depth interviewing used in this research was semistructured or focused interviewing.

The main selection criteria of interviewees were: (1) ease of access, (2) people closely involved in the operation of grants in impoverished Nationalist and Loyalist areas, (3) the extent to which the funded projects were deemed representative of promoting both intracommunity work and cross-community contact, and (4) a random representative sample of the funded community projects in Loyalist and Nationalist areas. Fourteen graduate students from Nova Southeastern University's Department of Conflict Analysis and Resolution, where I used to teach, assisted me with some of the field research component of the project—library research, interview scheduling, and other procedures.

One-on-one interviews were conducted over a three-month period during the summer of 1997, each lasting approximately 80–120 minutes. The interviewer and each participant had face-to-face contact at all times. Each interview was tape-recorded (the tape recorder placed to one side), analyzed, and inductive themes and coding categories determined (Smith 1995). I assured each person that no one would hear the tapes apart from me and my research assistants, and that all of the tapes would be destroyed after transcription.

Each participant was presented with the same five open-ended questions in which they had to comment on external economic aid, community development, and peace and reconciliation. No attempt was made to regulate the time spent on any particular question. This methodological tool allowed the participants to elaborate on what they perceived as the most important issues. For example, the participants were asked to explain differences between the IFI and EU Peace I funding processes, and whether these monies were contributing to the peace process. Probing the comments of participants led to a line of questions about the funding process and the role of funding that furnished valuable information.

I believe it is empowering to participants and their cultural context to present their exact words and expressions. All of the respondents clearly expressed their thoughts and ideas about each of the questions, and their assessments of both programs' overall framework were sophisticated and insightful. Every narrative presented in this study was transcribed verbatim and cited in its original form (with punctuation added to aid the "flow" of the spoken words into written text), which enabled participants' voices to be heard. Moreover, the lengthy quotes help to provide a deeper understanding of how the respondents critically evaluate international economic assistance in NI to discern what has worked, what has not, and

how economic assistance programs can be designed to have a more positive impact in conflict transformation.

The current study is a preliminary attempt to formulate hypotheses to
be tested in a further study of economic development and conflict resolution in Bosnia and Cyprus. While the data set is rich and complete,
and the narrative approach provides detailed information on the role of
external economic aid in revamping local economies in NI and along the
border with the Republic of Ireland, it is clear that new research is needed
if we are to completely understand the possible role of external economic
funding in promoting economic development in protracted ethnopolitical
conflicts. To that end, the NI data set stands out as an example for future
empirical analysis of economic development in conflict regions.

STUDIES OF ECONOMIC INITIATIVES IN NORTHERN IRELAND

In the past, the NI problem has not been high on the British government's
political agenda, and the government's major priority has been to limit the
cost of this involvement; thus its responses to economic inequality can be
described as superficial and palliative (Bew and Patterson 1985; Bew et al.
1995). During the 1970s, the aim of British economic policy was to bring
the Northern Irish economy into parity with the rest of the United Kingdom. The British government, belying an economist's understanding of the
roots of the conflict, invested massive infusions of cash in NI. However, this
economic subsidy addressed the symptoms and not the underlying causes
of the political and economic crisis (Irvin 1999; Morgan and Purdie 1980;
Munck 1985; Probert 1978; Rowthorn and Wayne 1988; Teague 1987).

The 1983 New Ireland Forum Report, which explicitly addressed the
relationship between economic deprivation, social and political marginalization, and support for the Nationalist and Loyalist paramilitary organizations, found that, "notwithstanding the attempts to remedy some of
the worst aspects of discrimination and the introduction of direct rule
from London in 1972, the structures in NI are such that Nationalists
are still discriminated against in social, economic, cultural and political
terms" (Callaghan14).

Building on the forum findings, the November 1985 Anglo-Irish
Agreement (AIA) created a framework for cross-border political and
economic cooperation between both parts of Ireland. To buttress its success, the AIA also established the IFI "to promote economic and social
advance, and to encourage contact, dialogue and reconciliation between
Nationalists and Unionists throughout Ireland" (5). During the 1985–88
period, the MacBride fair employment principles, which had been introduced in 1984 in response to continuing anti-Catholic discrimination,

were adopted in rapid succession by ten states in the American federation, which required divestiture of any investments in firms that did not adopt the principles. In NI, fifty-three American companies with a total of approximately eleven thousand employees, representing 10 percent of the manufacturing workforce and 2 percent of the total workforce, are now operating in accordance with the principles (Hevesi 1994)

The December 1993 Joint Declaration by the British and Irish prime ministers was instrumental in de-escalating the intercommunal conflict to such an extent as to facilitate the Provisional Irish Republican Army's (PIRA) cease-fire (Byrne 1995; O'Leary and McGarry 1993). Articles 24–38 of the subsequent February 1995 Joint Framework for Agreement Document proposed a North–South institutional body to formulate policies on an all-island basis. The agreement was designed to facilitate North–South harmonization on superordinate goals (agriculture, industrial development, transportation, energy, trade, health, education, and social welfare) through executive action in consultation with both governments (McGarry and O'Leary 1995). In response to this initiative, the EU established, in addition to its economic support through its structural funds, the EU Special Initiative for Peace and Reconciliation Agency, which provides funding for cross-border contact and development and community reconciliation projects. Similarly, the 1998 Good Friday Agreement stresses the importance of targeting marginalized communities for economic assistance from both the IFI and the EU Peace I Fund to promote self-esteem and empowerment, capacity building, and reconciliation across the bicommunal divide (Byrne and Ayulo 1998; Byrne and Irvin 2001, 2002; Irvin and Byrne 2002).

The stage is clearly set to facilitate intercommunal reconciliation, forge closer links between both parts of the island, entice economic investment in the region, and to nurture and sustain a peace process. Among the questions this project addresses precisely is the question of how policy makers within the contexts of negotiated agreements allocate tangible benefits deriving from the "peace dividend" to sustain domestic political support for the peace process.

THE INTERNATIONAL FUND FOR IRELAND AND THE EUROPEAN UNION PEACE FUNDS

The International Fund for Ireland

As introduced earlier, the International Fund for Ireland was created in September 1986 by the British and Irish governments, based on objectives stated in Article 10(a) of the Anglo-Irish Agreement of 1985:

The two Governments shall cooperate to promote the economic and social development of those areas of both parts of Ireland, which have suffered most severely from the consequences of the instability of recent years, and shall consider the possibility of securing international support for this work.

The language of the law authorizing the United States' contribution makes clear the relationship the U.S. administration and Congress perceived between peace and economic development.

The purpose of this Act is to provide for the United States contributions in support of the Anglo-Irish Agreement, such contributions to consist of economic support fund assistance for payment to the International Fund . . . as well as other assistance to serve as an incentive for economic development and reconciliation in Ireland and NI . . . in which all may live in peace, free from discrimination, terrorism, and intolerance and with the opportunity for both communities to participate fully in the structures and processes of government.

Successive U.S. administrations and the U.S. Congress have continued to view economic development as a key to fostering peace in NI. As support for both Republican and Loyalist paramilitaries has traditionally been strongest in those communities that suffer the highest level of unemployment and economic deprivation, many advocates of the IFI view the creation of jobs and economic opportunity as an essential component in reaching a solution to the political conflict in NI (Irvin 1999). The following comments made by Senator Patrick Leahy (1995, 2917) regarding the fund underscore this sentiment:

Lasting peace means urgently dealing with the terrible problem of unemployment in the North. People need to have confidence in their government, but they also need jobs; they need economic security as well as physical security . . . I am reminded of what Senator Mitchell, quoting Franklin Roosevelt said to an audience in Dublin: "In the dark days of our Great Depression," President Roosevelt said, "the only thing we have to fear is fear itself." He also said, "the best social program is a job." (Cited in Irvin and Byrne 2002, 134)

As table 1 indicates, financial support for the IFI from the United States, while not on the same level as aid provisions to other conflict-torn areas such as the Palestinian Authority, nevertheless has remained relatively constant since its initial seed funding (Brynen 2000). U.S. funds pledged as of November 1996 reached $500 million, and EU funds pledged (excluding those from the European Investment Bank) reached $300 million (Irvin and Byrne 2002).

Table 1. U.S. Contribution to the IFI, 1986–2007

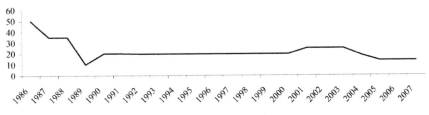

Adapted from Irvin and Byrne 2002, 134.

Other donors to the IFI include the European Union, Canada, New Zealand, and Australia. Since 1989, the EU has contributed approximately $18.3 million per year. In response to the 1994 cease-fires, the EU has increased its annual contribution to approximately $24.4 million per year supplanting the United States as the largest donor to the fund (Irvin and Byrne 2002).

IFI annual reports tended to paint a rather optimistic picture of the fund's grant activities. For example, the IFI's 2004 annual report stated that,

> Over the last 18 years, since 1986, the IFI has promoted economic and social advance and encouraged contact, dialogue and reconciliation between Nationalists and Unionists throughout Ireland by providing financial assistance to a wide range of projects. . . . To date, the Fund has committed some 527 m to over 5,500 projects that have promoted economic development and social advance in disadvantaged areas and contributed to making progress in cross community reconciliation. The results of this work can be seen in almost every city, town and village in NI and in the border counties of the south. (IFI 2004, 6)

However, in the early days concerns arose in the U.S. Congress that American tax dollars were being channeled into white elephant projects such as refurbishing banks rather than neglected and disadvantaged areas, thereby excluding members of the community (Brett 1990, 436). In addition, Protestant Unionist leaders, such as the Reverend Ian Paisley, perceived the IFI as Irish American blood money that discriminated against Protestant Unionists by providing more resources in Catholic Nationalist areas (Byrne and Irvin 2001, 2002) where they were discouraged from applying for grants to the IFI. As a result, Protestant Unionists began to feel alienated, disenfranchised, and hostile (KPMG 1995).

Despite these initial setbacks, independent assessments of the IFI glowingly reported that "the IFI remains the largest single source for cross-border development" (KPMG 1995, 16), "which is able to target disadvantage, and social exclusion by creating private investment in disadvantaged communities and by targeting cross-community and cross-border divisions" (KPMG 2001, 9). Similarly, reports by the European Commission and the European Court of Auditors highlighted the IFI's positive track record in promoting socioeconomic advance and in encouraging contact between Unionists and Nationalists (European Court of Auditors 2000).

The European Union Peace Funds

Northern Ireland and the Republic of Ireland also receive substantial EU assistance through the EU structural funds for economically depressed regions and the Special Support Program for Peace and Reconciliation in Ireland (EU Peace I Fund) (Byrne and Ayulo 1998, 421–24). During the period 1989–94, NI received over one billion European currency units (ECU) from the European structural funds.

The EU Peace I Fund was an initiative of the former president of the European Commission Jacques Delors, introduced in the weeks following the announcements of the Provisional Irish Republican Army (PIRA) and Combined Loyalist Military Command (CLMC) cease-fire in the autumn of 1994. It promised 300 million ECU ($393 million) for the period 1995–98 (Byrne and Irvin 2001). The European Commission has since proposed over $220 million additional funds. Together with the structural funds applied to the Republic of Ireland, the EU will have invested over 1.2 billion ECU by the year 2000 in the island of Ireland. As stated in its program summary, the strategic objectives of the Peace Fund were: (1) "to reinforce progress towards a peaceful and stable society and to promote reconciliation by increasing economic development and employment, promoting urban and rural regeneration, developing cross-border cooperation and extending social inclusion, (2) to promote the social inclusion of those at the margins of economic and social life, and (3) to exploit the opportunities and address the needs arising from the peace process in order to boost economic growth and stimulate social and economic regeneration" (EU Court of Auditors 2000).

The Peace Fund has supported a large number of projects in the areas of economy, employment, educational disadvantage, and social inclusion. Its focus on poverty, economic development, and social inclusion (issues that, failing to address them cause and perpetuate violence) empowered the grass roots to be involved in the transformation of NI's society and the border area (Harvey 2003). The Peace I Program or Fund created Intermediary Funding Bodies (IFBs) to administer small seeding grants and district partnerships that provided funding to community groups who had previously not received funding. These "had a greater impact as they enabled the building of previously nonexistent capacity within many communities. . . . Real change required a bottom-up approach, which small seeding grants more than encouraged" (Buchanan 2005, 26). The empowerment of the grass roots was critical for the overall success of the program (Coopers and Lybrand 1997).

The design of the EU Peace I Program or Fund involved input from local politicians, the community, voluntary sectors, and NI's three MEPs (member of the European Parliament) to create a cross-community rather than a sectarian approach to economic development and reconciliation (EU Court of Auditors 2000). The relationship was stronger between social inclusion and economic regeneration (Peace I Fund) and peace and reconciliation (Peace II Fund). For example, the district partnerships brought together a plethora of socioeconomic and political interest groups across society to cocreate inclusive and focused development plans (PricewaterhouseCoopers 2003). In addition, in contrast to the Unionist Protestant community, the Nationalist Catholic community had established local structures that enabled them to tap into the funds (Paisley, Hume, and Nicholson 1997).

However, there were a number of problems with the EU Peace I Fund. Harvey's (1997) critique of Peace I was that it was hurriedly put together without a clear understanding of what socioeconomic and political core issues needed to be addressed to free up innovative peace building approaches. Moreover, it was noted that the complicated application forms and requirements, as well as unclear program and monitoring information, complicated the application process (Paisley, Hume, and Nicholson 1997).

THE ROLE OF ECONOMIC ASSISTANCE IN BUILDING THE PEACE DIVIDEND IN ETHNOPOLITICAL CONFLICTS

A central premise of this project is that international economic assistance exerts important but underexamined influences upon both intra- and interethnic relations in divided societies (Esman 1991, 1995, 1997). Since much ethnic conflict is rooted in competition for scarce resources, international assistance, in terms of both funding and policy recommendations, can obviously influence both economic and social development. At present, however, empirical studies of the dynamic process of interactive formation or reformulation of ethnic identities resulting from economic changes driven by international forces remain scarce (Brynen 2000). As mentioned above, building on the work of Esman (1991, 1995, 1997) and Lederach (1997), this study specifically (1) describes the respondents' ideas about the contribution of economic assistance to peace and reconciliation; (2) examines the respondents' view of the relationship of economic assistance to economic regeneration, community development, and empowerment; and (3) interprets the respondents' images about the role of economic assistance in intracommunity work and in building cross-community ties.

External economic assistance is important for capacity building and in building the peace dividend (Byrne and Irvin 2002). External economic assistance from international agencies can create opportunities for people in the grass roots that can then empower them to start up indigenous businesses for themselves. It is an important component of constructive conflict resolution because it also promotes partnerships between local communities, nongovernmental organizations (NGOs), and governments. External economic assistance foments a new, creative way of thinking about economic recovery after the war and promotes responsibility and accountability for action. For example, the EU Peace I Fund and the IFI have actively promoted the peace dividend (Byrne and Ayulo 1998; Byrne and Irvin 2000), by channeling economic aid to impoverished regions in NI to promote capacity building, grassroots entrepreneurs, and reconciliation.

However, it is important to note that the European Court of Auditors found that the IFI's evaluation of project applications and postgrant monitoring of projects did not "ensure sound financial management in all cases," whereas the EU's Peace I Program's selection and appraisal procedures "lacked common criteria," and an "effective methodology" for targeting community projects and social groups (EU Court of Auditors 2000, 11–12). Similarly, as cited earlier, Harvey's report on the EU's Peace I Program suggested a need for more rigor in program design to devise appropriate indicators and measures to monitor the program's peacebuilding effectiveness (Harvey 1997, 84). Comments like these support my contention that a study identifying and analyzing recipients' perceptions about a program's effectiveness is both important and timely.

Virtually every country in the world—developing or developed—is facing the prospect of some form of ethnic conflict within or transcending its borders (Pearson 2001; Sandole 2002). Today we can see the difficulty faced by the international community in winning the peace in postconflict Iraq, preventing a resurgence of ethnic violence in failed nation-states in Burundi, Haiti, Rwanda, and Sudan, and negotiating an end to civil wars in the Congo, Sierra Leone, Sri Lanka, and elsewhere. In the face of these other ethnic conflicts, understanding the effect of external economic assistance in building the peace dividend in NI is valuable in its own right. Potentially, it is also of practical use to donor agencies and policy makers. Northern Ireland provides a historical perspective to guide both internal and external policy, particularly in the context of external economic assistance to postconflict societies, which must now come to terms with this process. Most donors are guided by the assumption that promoting economic development enhances the prospects for peace by bridging ethnopolitical divisions, empowering communities, and encouraging the de-escalation of conflict.

According to data compiled from the Organization of Economic Cooperation and Development (OECD), countries emerging from conflict received aid commitments of approximately $109 billion from multilateral institutions and development assistance committee members (OECD 1999). As donor agencies have become increasingly involved in postconflict peace building, there has evolved a greater awareness of the fact that the inequalities that block the prospects for peace include class, race, ethnicity, religions, and region (Boyce 2000, 374). Increasingly, the economic policies that have exacerbated these later cleavages have been identified as significant causes of the violent civil wars and their remedy a key component in postconflict peace building.

CONCLUSIONS

In this study I identify how the recipients of international postconflict peace-building assistance, and members of the public themselves, perceive the politics and the possibilities of that aid in promoting and sustaining postconflict reconciliation and economic reconstruction. Specifically, this study analyzes how the respondents think about external economic funding from the IFI and the EU Peace I Fund. In particular, I am interested in how and whether they perceive both funds playing an important socioeconomic and political role in addressing structural inequality and in promoting both single-identity work and cross-cultural contact and reconciliation between Protestant Unionists and Catholic Nationalists in NI and the border counties. I suggest that this analysis provides important findings that can uniquely inform donor agencies, and in particular, their representatives on the ground regarding the symbolic as well as the objective considerations of their economic intervention in conflict and postconflict situations.

2

The Northern Ireland Conflict: Analysis and Resolution

INTRODUCTION

FOLLOWING ELECTIONS HELD ON MARCH 7, 2007, the Democratic Unionist Party (DUP) and Sinn Féin (SF) agreed on a political arrangement that allows for the restoration of the Northern Ireland Assembly, which had been suspended since 2002. On March 26, 2007, during historic talks at Stormont, the ten-year protracted peace process resulted in face-to-face talks between Ian Paisley and Gerry Adams to agree on a date for the return of power sharing in Northern Ireland. On May 8, 2007, power was transferred from London to the Belfast Assembly with the Reverend Ian Paisley and Martin McGuinness of SF nominated as first minister and deputy first minister, respectively, and with the 108-member assembly's four largest parties nominating ten departmental ministers. We live in interesting times!

However, as the history of other ethnic conflicts illustrates, the politics of consensus can be dangerous. In Cyprus and Lebanon, for example, institutionalized consociational power sharing was exploited by political leaders to create stalemate and sectarian ethnic divisions that eventually fragmented into ethnic warfare (Byrne 2000, 2007; McGarry and O'Leary 2004). Thus, there is a need for NI's citizens and other political actors—the Official Unionist Party (OUP), the Social Democratic and Labour Party (SDLP), the Green Party, and the Women's Coalition—to be actively involved in "peace imagining" (Boulding 2000) to create a "moral imagination" (Lederach 2005) and to put forward policy papers and new creative ideas so as not to freeze sectarian politics.

Moreover, South Africa has inspired the divided and war-weary communities in NI to embrace the compromises of politics (Guelke 1988, 2000). The African National Congress (ANC) and Nelson Mandela mentored Gerry Adams and senior Republicans to reach out to Unionists as well, putting pressure on the British government to include Republicans in the peace process while the United States and both external ethnoguarantors—the Irish and British governments—nurtured the peace process along (Byrne 2007).

Consequently, the new seismic political shifts taking shape in NI's politics suggests that both communities, especially the Unionist majority and Irish Republicans have taken major leaps of faith to transform the conflict.

The 1998 Good Friday Agreement also brought Loyalists and Republicans in from the cold, reformed the police to become a more representative body when dealing with Loyalist parades along the Ormeau and Garvaghy roads, and brought Unionists and Nationalists to the negotiating table and into a devolved power-sharing government (Cox 1999).

This chapter uses the social cubism analytical model to highlight the interaction of material and psychological mechanisms that shape and affect the dynamics of the NI conflict. Six dimensions or factors combine to produce patterns of interethnic behavior.

SOCIAL CUBISM

Social cubism is an analytical framework that includes six interrelated factors—history, religion, politics, psychocultural, demographics, and economics—that produce multiple relationships, patterns, and events (Byrne and Carter 1996). The interrelationships among the six sides operate simultaneously and reproduce, integrate, and change over time, space, and context within plasmic, complex, and compressed social conflicts (Byrne, Carter, and Senehi 2003).

1. Historical Factors

1. PAST HISTORICAL EVENTS

When they interpret the past, Protestants and Catholics emphasize different historical events in their historical narratives. "Collective memories" leads to the reinterpretation of historical events, such as the Famine and Bloody Sunday, in a process of "time collapse," where past and present become fused as one (Volkan 1998). For example, on July 12, Protestants celebrate the 1690 Battle of Boyne when William of Orange defeated the Catholic English king, James II, while Catholics celebrate the 1916 Rising during Easter week (Byrne 2002). Consequently, the "transgenerational transmission of trauma" exists where each historical tragedy is passed from one generation to the next as part of each group's "victim mentality" (Volkan 1998). Integrated schools help to reframe and refocus history to improve understanding and communication between Protestants and Catholics (Byrne 1997).

2. EXCLUSION AND INDEPENDENCE

Protestant and Catholic communities each perceive themselves as independent of the other. Each group's historical framework is rigidified

through the historical re-creation of events that produce a set of characteristics that define group membership. For example, Protestants believe
that during the 1916 Battle of the Somme they signed their covenant to
the queen with their blood sacrifice on the fields of France (Byrne 1997),
and during the marching season each summer they march to mark out
territory. The 1603 Flight of the Earls and the 1692 apartheid Penal
Laws prevented Catholics from practicing their religion, speaking the
Gaelic language, being elected to public office, and bequeathing private
property, and these events are enshrined in the collective folklore of the
Nationalist community (Byrne and Carter 1996). Catholic insurrection
and Protestant resistance continued until the 1921 partition of Ireland. In
NI Protestants and Catholics have coexisted uneasily ever since.

3. GENDER AND INEQUALITY

In NI patriarchy has framed the historical narrative in terms of a male
power and privilege that generally excludes women's voices (Smith 2003).
During the Troubles, Republican and Loyalist paramilitary women were
rarely part of Active Service Units (ASUs). Except for the People's Democracy peace movement led by Betty Williams and Mairead Corrigan,
women remain largely relegated to the margins of mainstream politics.

4. DESTRUCTIVE STORIES

Both communities have strong and opposing stories of the past. As
destructive stories inform people's perceptions about current events
(Senehi 1996, 2000), a local folklore has built up in each community
about the conflict and the atrocities carried out by the "other" side as well
as the goodness and glory of each group. As a result of these stories, fear,
suspicion, and threat evoke a demonization and hatred of the "other"
side, and in the segregated schools children perceive the other community as evil (Byrne 1997).

5. GOLDEN AGE

Each ethnic group looks into its past to find its golden age for a sense of
efficacy, identity, belonging, and value in the present (Smith 2003). For
example, Protestant Unionists evoke a sense of pride in building up the
agricultural and economic base of Ulster during the seventeenth century.
Ulster's linen mills supplied the British economy with goods while the Har-
land and Wolf shipbuilding yards created some of the finest oceangoing
ships—the *Titanic* for one—ever built. On the other hand, Catholic Nationalists trace their roots back to the golden age of the Celts and Vikings up

until the twelfth century when the Normans established a military presence in Ireland that conquered the Gaelic chieftains (Byrne 1997).

6. DIVIDED COMMUNITIES, DIVIDED STORIES

Segregated schools and textbooks ensure that children grow up in a divided society. In addition, segregated neighborhoods are territorially defensible and preserve each community's way of life as sectarianism locks both communities in ethnic strife (Byrne 2000). Intensified polarization between these divided communities has frustrated political attempts to accommodate both traditions (Byrne 1995). For example, Tony Blair's Bloody Sunday Inquiry has opened up a lot of old wounds in Derry.

2. Religious Factors

1. INTERFAITH DIALOGUE

The process of interfaith dialogue expressed through the leaders of the Presbyterian, Methodist, Church of Ireland, and Catholic churches encouraged NI's politicians to work toward a devolved power-sharing government. The October 9, 2006, meeting between delegations led by Catholic archbishop Brady and the Reverend Ian Paisley, head of the Protestant Democratic Unionist Party, was an important milestone in the normalization of intercommunal relations.

2. TRUE BELIEVERS

In NI some emphasize that religion is a key boundary or identity marker in distinguishing between both ethnic protagonists (Guelke 2004; McGarry and O'Leary 2007), while others see religion as significant because of special circumstances (Bruce 1986; Elliot 2000). "True Believers" believe their religion is the only true religion as they are God's chosen people with a divine right to the land. In the process they construct other believers as savage and uncivilized (Smith 2003). Ian Paisley's Free Presbyterian Church believes that the Catholic religion is the Antichrist, so how can Protestants share power with Catholics? Catholics and Protestants believe that each has a legitimacy and right to hold the territory, and they use stereotypes to construct the other. Conflicts that arise over the nature of the NI state may help the Protestant and Catholic communities to socialize, thereby increasing group identity and augmenting group structure. Conflict is a dynamic process that the parties both control and are controlled by. Accordingly, while one group may manipulate the tensions produced by stereotypes of their community to ensure that their members do not cross the sectarian divide, this conflict may discourage the other group from having any form of contact with that group, thus impeding overall relations (Wright 1987).

3. SEGREGATION AND POLARIZATION

Segregation and polarization prevent the development of a comprehensive third pillar to transform relationships. The mixed marriage rate in NI is well below 5 percent (Arthur 2000). There is little contact since people live in segregated neighborhoods, patronize different stores, read different newspapers, and attend different churches and schools, all of which reinforce and sustain the conflict (Darby 1976, 2001).

4. BADGE OF IDENTITY

In NI religion is a badge of identity or a cultural marker rather than a direct cause of the conflict (Whyte 1990). In the bipolar society of NI, it is critical to one's safety to be able to figure out who the other is—through pronouncing the letter H or the "H-Test," first and last names, neighborhoods, and "spotting" (ibid.). The 1885–86 and 1918 general elections in Ireland placed the dominant national question at center stage with Protestants supporting Unionism and Catholics tied to Nationalism (Coakley 1996). Thus, Nationalism and religion strengthened and reinforced each other in NI as separate ethnic identities developed into a strongly segregated society (Darby 1976).

5. INTRAGROUP CONFLICT

Professor John Whyte used to say, "When we talk about the conflict, which Catholics and which Protestants are we talking about?" Intragroup conflict exists in both communities between moderates and extremists (Byrne and Delman 1999). The Catholic community is fairly homogenous and the Protestant community is heterogeneous, except in a crisis when the Protestant community bands together to resist the perceived political threat (Byrne 1997). Certainly, in the past moderates were afraid to reach across the bicommunal divide to like-minded individuals. Paramilitary punishment beatings and shootings instill fear and prevent cross-community contact.

6. SECTARIANISM AND FEAR OF OSTRACISM

Religious belief has infused the conflict over national identities, and since the political parties have structural and ideological links to their respective religious communities (Guelke 2004) has encouraged sectarianism. Sectarianism was built into socioeconomic and political institutions by the Protestant Unionist elite to keep the working classes divided (Bew et al. 1979, 1995). Lingering sectarian tensions and segregation are exemplified by continued attacks on new immigrants to NI as the breakaway Orange Defenders and Real Irish Republican Army (RIRA) threaten the peace process. Northern Irish people have generally welcomed peace; however, devolution is based on policing people apart, which reinforces segregation by insisting that both communities are represented by politicians who advocate for their own group against the other group for limited resources (Dixon 2007). Religion is an ideological belief system that provides a sense of identity and security with historical roots for both communities (Mitchel 2003). It is difficult to step outside of one's kin group as religion and loyalty to one's ethnonational identity are intertwined (English 2004).

3. Political Factors

1. EXCLUSION FROM POWER

The Catholic-Protestant cleavage in NI is very sharp politically. The very existence of the state is the central political question, perhaps because economic setbacks and resulting decreases in the standard of living do little to enhance the internal legitimacy and acceptance of NI by Catholic Nationalists (Byrne 2001a, 2001b). When Ireland was partitioned by the 1920 Government of Ireland Act, a perceived disloyal Catholic minority was excluded from the political process. In 1921 James Craig, the first NI prime minister (PM) described this process "as a Protestant state for a Protestant people" with Protestant Unionists voting for pro-British parties and Catholics for pro-Nationalist and Republican political parties (Byrne 1997). From 1920 to 1972, a Populist Unionist government excluded Catholics as an effective opposition in Stormont (Bew et al. 1979, 1995). During the 1960s an empowered Catholic community used nonviolent civil disobedience to assert their socioeconomic and political rights (Arthur 2000).

John Hume and the Northern Ireland Civil Rights Association movement (NICRA) effectively sent the state into convulsions and chaos as the situation quickly spiraled into a polarized sectarian conflict (Arthur 2000). The emergence of the NICRA movement reflected a rising Catholic professional class that was prepared to move toward integration, thus allaying "irredentist irreconcilability to give way to serious political activity" (Farrell 1980, 64). It was the development of NICRA along with the parallel impulse of a strong Republican movement that began to make itself felt more strongly after August 1969, setting the stage for the events that led to direct rule in 1972 (Bew et al. 1995). Thus, the immediate impact for reform in the mid- to late 1960s was political and not purely economic, explaining why the movement should have a more enduring popular impact among the Catholic working class (Bew et al. 1995).

The NICRA movement's ability to mobilize such popular support in 1968–69 was due to the emergence of the British Labour Party, perceived by Catholics as sympathetic to their grievances (Farrell 1983). Also, the deferential response of the old Catholic Nationalist party to O'Neillism was an important political factor that had a bearing upon Catholic mobilization (McGarry and O'Leary 1995). The instantaneous popularity of the movement seems to be due largely to the Unionists' institutionalization of exclusivism, which led to economic and political grievances over status among the Catholic middle class and the steady augmentation of a reservoir of potential support for extreme politics among unskilled Catholic workers (Bew et al. 1979). Socialism failed to unite the Protestant and Catholic working class once the nature of the state became prominent again with the emergence of the Provisional Irish Republican Army (PIRA) as a military force in the Catholic areas. Thus, when the powder keg ignited, the British government had no alternative but to send in the troops.

2. MINORITY SCAPEGOATING

As Catholics were perceived as a disloyal fifth column (Dixon 2000), the political legitimacy of NI fostered sectarian politics. Northern Ireland turned its legal and political institutions against the Catholic minority with the creation of the B Specials and the 1920 Special Powers Act, which gave draconian powers to this quasi-paramilitary force (Farrell 1983). Protestant Unionists sought to maintain peace through security and safeguard Protestant heritage and identity and NI's constitutional status as part of the United Kingdom (Farrell 1980). Competition over contested boundaries led to minority scapegoating by Protestants who lived in a perpetual state of siege (Byrne 1995). The failure of the nonviolent NICRA movement to secure the same socioeconomic and political privileges for the Catholic community encouraged the political violence of the PIRA and the determination of the Protestant community to protect the British link (Byrne 2007).

3. POLITICAL INSTITUTIONS

The apartheid Penal Laws of the seventeenth century were repealed by Daniel O'Connell in 1820. As religion became superimposed on the national question, the Home Rule crisis of the late nineteenth century was interpreted by Protestants as Rome Rule, resulting in the establishment in 1912 of the Ulster Volunteer Force (UVF) (Byrne and Carter 1996). The 1916 Rising and the subsequent 1919–21 War of Independence carried out by Michael Collins's Irish Republican Army (IRA) resulted in a truce and negotiations with British PM Lloyd George's coalition government, which resulted in the Irish Free State, partition, and a vicious civil war between pro- and anti-Treaty factions of the IRA (Byrne 1997).

In NI from 1922 to 1972, the gerrymandering of local and national electoral boundaries and franchise restrictions prevented Catholics from being elected to Stormont, ensuring that Nationalists were not properly represented at either the local government or the parliamentary level (Arthur 2000). Ultimately Protestants are loyal to the queen as titular head of the British state and head of the Church of England, while government lacks the religious legitimacy of the monarch (Byrne and Carter 1996). Today there are little crosscutting cleavages between the political parties who remain divided over the national question.

4. NATIONALISM

Christianity has influenced the invention and reinvention of nationalism in Ireland (Comerford 2003). The NI conflict is intractable because two separate identities are competing for the same territory, enhancing feelings of fear, suspicion, and uncertainty that shape the political agenda of both communities (Byrne, Carter, and Senehi 2003). The decline of traditional Nationalism is best exemplified by the rapid decline of the pro-GFA Nationalist Social Democratic and Labour Party. In the political game to win the hearts and minds of urban and rural Catholic grassroots politics (Byrne 2001a, 2001b), the slick electoral machine politics of SF successfully outmaneuvered the SDLP in constituency development. However, for now, SF has given up its historical claim to a free united Ireland as the Belfast Assembly guarantees that NI remains part of the UK. Sinn Féin and the PIRA fought to remove the British presence from Ireland for good, but now accept that NI will remain part of Britain until a future majority in NI decides to opt out of the UK and reunify the island (Byrne 2007). Sinn Féin's switch to the strategy of the politics of birthrates—when Catholics in NI eventually outbreed Protestants and can vote for an independent Ireland along with new immigrants from Eastern European countries within the European Union such as Poland, Slovakia, and Lithuania—has ensured that for now SF supports and will advocate for a policy for the equal treatment and respect of Catholics within NI (Byrne 2007).

The 1998 Good Friday Agreement led to a successful negotiation to establish a devolved power-sharing administration while rogue militants from the UVF, the Ulster Defense Association (UDA), and the PIRA oppose the political deal. Partition and the border remain as the key issues in the conflict (Byrne 2002). A combination of British strategies to defeat the PIRA, accommodate moderate Catholics, and neutralize the Unionist veto has undercut traditional Unionism represented by the Official Unionist Party and reactionary Unionism embodied by the DUP (Dixon 2007). Extremist Unionists within the DUP and Loyalist paramilitaries have not forced the British government to remain in NI against its will. For example, as the government abandoned the Unionists to strengthen British interests within NI, the Unionist veto was culled from the political landscape by PM Margaret Thatcher and the 1985 Anglo-Irish Agreement (McGarry and O'Leary 2007). Moreover, the decline of traditional Unionism represented by the spectacular demise of the OUP over the past five years occurred as Unionists voted for the DUP in contrast to the OUP because it clearly articulated their interests (Ryan 2007).

5. PARAMILITARIES

During the Troubles, Republican and Loyalist violence targeted civilians in addition to the security forces, thereby producing a state of fear as well as a self-perpetuating pattern of deterrence and revenge (Byrne and Carter 1996). Sectarian violence polarized both communities, reinforcing fears of genocide in both communities. Initially formed to protect their communities, rival paramilitaries took the "long war" to the enemy. The PIRA, armed with Libyan weapons, adopted "the armalite and ballot box" dual strategy while the Loyalist paramilitaries, supplied with munitions by the South African Defense Force (SADF), carried out a strategy of the targeted assassination of suspected PIRA personnel and Catholic civilians (Byrne 1995; Guelke 1988). In the aftermath of the PIRA and Combined Loyalist Military Command, reciprocal cease-fires in 1994 paramilitary violence (in the form of local punishment beatings) have continued (Darby and MacGinty 2000), while rogue Loyalists and Republicans have detached themselves from the PIRA, UDA, and UVF (Byrne 2002).

6. SECURITY POLICY

In 1921 the Unionist government's lack of trust in Britain's long-term intentions toward NI made necessary the maximum possible degree of Unionist unity, which further meant introducing a draconian array of repressive legislation against the Nationalist minority (Bew et al. 1979; Farrell 1980). This new NI administration placed increasing reliance on the sectarian Royal Ulster Constabulary (RUC) and a Special Constabulary under local control (the B Specials) responsive to local Protestant pressures and used effectively in policing the Nationalist community (Farrell 1983). The adoption of a more strident anti-Catholic position by Unionist politicians was part of the same strategy for maximizing Protestant unity (Wright 1973; O'Leary and McGarry 1993). Discrimination was an ongoing process, and as Bew et al. (1979, 1995) have argued, deliberately designed to reproduce the privileges of the Protestant population. The B Specials were used to protect the local Protestant community against what they perceived to be potentially overt hostile aggression that would be directed against them by Catholics.

With the collapse of the Unionist regime in 1972, due to the escalation of violence the British government implemented a policy of criminalization to end "Special Category Status" for Republican and Loyalist prisoners. A policy of containment ensured that an "acceptable level of violence" was the norm, while the policy of "Ulsterization" placed the RUC and the Ulster Defense Regiment (UDR) on the front line in the long war with the PIRA (Bew and Patterson 1985). The effects of these security policies were the 1982 hunger strikes, the Supergrass informant system, the no-jury three-judge Diplock courts, and a "shoot-to-kill" policy by the Special Airborne Service (SAS) and RUC special branch (McGarry and O'Leary 2004).

4. Psychocultural Factors

1. IDENTITY

Group identity assists Protestants and Catholics to develop a sense of self-esteem that requires a sense of belonging and a sense of differentiation from the other community (Byrne 2001a). Two opposing ethnic identities competing for the same territory leads to the intractability of the NI conflict (Byrne and Carter 1996). As both communities portray the other culture as the out-group (Byrne 2001b), tensions have often escalated conflict during political crises or perceived social change in NI. Cultural symbols reinforce group solidarity and identity while stereotypes of the other flourish (Byrne 1995). Thus, British and Irish identities exclude those who do not fit within the cultural traits of the in-group and perpetrate a sense of ethnocentrism as subjective factors are inextricably tied to the objective interests (Senehi 2000).

2. IN-GROUP-OUT-GROUP

Both ethnic groups in NI attribute positive traits and values to their own group—portraying themselves as brave, courageous, determined, hardworking, and intelligent—and using stereotypes to frame the other (Byrne and Ayulo 1998). This is why the late Frank Wright used to say to his class that stereotypes need to be challenged empirically on a day-to-day basis. Both Catholics and Protestants perceive the social situation in determining the nature of their interrelations in NI. The more Catholics perceive society to be dichotomized, the more they feel themselves to be targets of adverse discrimination (Byrne 1995). This serves to influence how they interpret events at the local level, which in turn helps to reinforce the view of society being dichotomized (ibid.). This awareness of major political differences at the national level is crucial. It results in ideology structuring experience rather than experience structuring one's ideology. The end result is that the ideology of one community determines its views on the condition and aspirations of the other community, and hence, whether to decide on the desirability or otherwise of cooperating with them (Wright 1996). This belief structure is fundamental in the economic sphere.

The underlying reality in NI is the reproduction of the state, the reproduction of the objective conditions upon which the ideology rested (Byrne 2001a, 2001b). Ideology itself is a reflection and interpretation of reality and corresponds to what the individual, whether Catholic or Protestant, experiences in his or her daily life. Thus, rather than simply structuring experience, ideology is shaped by it. Catholics in NI did represent a threat to Protestants, not merely economically but politically and religiously as well. It was this threat that shaped the ideology of Protestants, not the other way around (Bew 2007). Catholics and Protestants do hold exaggerated fears of each other, and this cannot be overcome while both communities remain divided over the legitimacy of the state. What is important is the relationship of both communities to each other and their relationship with the state.

3. THE MEDIA'S DISTORTION OF THE OTHER

Even the media in NI is dichotomized—distorting images of the other community, rejecting compromise, and creating an intense hostility and imagery. Nationalists read the *Irish News* and watch Radio Telifís Éireann (RTÉ) while Unionists subscribe to the *Belfast Telegraph* and the British Broadcasting Corporation (BBC). Sinn Féin publishes *An Phoblacht,* which is patronized by Republicans, while Loyalists read *Combat,* produced by the UVF. The media focuses on outrageous behavior and instills a "fear of genocide," anger, and frustration within both communities. For example, sectarian murders, pogroms, and kneecapping are used as each group's self-presentation of being victims of the other side (McGarry 2001).

4. PERCEPTIONS AND SIEGE MENTALITY

Myths of siege, massacre, martyrdom, and victory shape both cultural traditions and coexist uneasily in a sectarian environment (Byrne 1999). Historical events thus serve to promote group solidarity as symbolic rituals foster sectarian belief structures and further escalate the conflict (Byrne 2007). Republican violence and Catholicism is centered on Christlike martyrs—Bobby Sands and Padraig Pearse—and the redemptive nature of a blood sacrifice (Byrne and Carter 1996). Each act of the other group is interpreted in negative terms, which serves to escalate tensions between both groups. Thus, Protestant Unionists perceive that they are a besieged community constantly under attack from Catholic Nationalists. In the past "No Surrender" and "Not an Inch" were the slogans of the Unionist community. The insurrection of Catholics and Protestant resistance through the UVF of 1912 and 1975 are shaped by these perceptions of siege mentality.

5. CULTURAL SYMBOLS AND RITUALS

Protestants and Catholics invoke ethnonational and political issues representative of group traditions that promote stereotyping and prejudice (McGarry 2001). Economic and political issues are complicated by national identity crises shrouded in cultural symbols and rituals that make the NI conflict appear intractable. Cultural markers such as flags, national anthems, holidays, language, dress, custom, sports, and cultural events (for example, Irish Fleadh Cheoil's) mark out group boundaries and serve to reinforce group identity (Whyte 1990). Consequently, Orange parades are perceived by Protestants as a cultural event and a right to "walk the Queen's highway," and by Catholics as triumphalism. Likewise Easter lilies commemorating the 1916 Easter Rising reinforce Catholic Nationalist in-group solidarity and out-group hostility to Protestant Unionists.

6. VOLUNTARY AND FORCED SEGREGATION

During the 1960s and 1970s people were burned out of mixed neighborhoods and lived within their own enclaves to protect their "way of life" and some kind of cultural tranquillity (Wright 1987). In NI Protestants and Catholics remain, for the most part, segregated, living in single-identity neighborhoods, attending separate churches and schools, and rarely intermarrying across the bicommunal divide (Mitchell 2006). Consequently, an adverse effect upon the development of socialism is the divisiveness and antagonisms between Protestantism and Catholicism that have inhibited unity along class lines and contributed to sectarianism

(Byrne 2006). This religious division was increased and deepened by the problem of partition, which contributed to the strength of Nationalism and Unionism over socialism (Byrne 2000).

5. Demographic Factors

1. DOUBLE MINORITY AND DOUBLE MAJORITY

Catholic Nationalists are a majority on the island of Ireland and a minority in NI, while Protestants are a majority in NI but a minority on the island. Both ethnic groups are minorities within the UK and EU contexts, perceive themselves as minorities, and are viewed by the other community as a threatening majority (Byrne and Carter 1996). The possibility of a united Ireland threatens Protestants who, as a besieged community, defend themselves against both internal and external assault (Whyte 1990). The accelerated birth rate in the Catholic community increases Protestant fears of an eventual united Ireland that they perceive as hostile to their identity and interests (Dixon 2007).

Shifting geographic contexts have important psychological as well as political ramifications, since an ethnic group that is a majority can suddenly become a minority and vice versa. Thus, whoever controls the territory and the resources has critical implications for both ethnic communities. In NI during the late 1980s, the British government began to nurture and support organizations in the grass roots that fostered intercommunal contact and dialogue (Byrne 2001a, 2001b). For example, the Community Relations Council (CRC) was established in 1990 by the British government to assist grassroots organizations in both communities to develop relationships at any level in the overall society (Arthur 2000). The CRC assists employers and staff within an organization or trade union group to take steps to redress discriminatory behavior. The goal of the CRC's antisectarian work is not to change the attitudes of the workers but to change the work practice.

2. INTRAGROUP CONFLICT

Intragroup conflict in NI over the use of political violence and political accommodation makes compromise difficult and reduces the potential to create a shared identity (Ryan 2007). When it comes to defining the group's relationship with the other community, conflict escalates within both groups with extremists censuring and marginalizing moderates. Today the extremist political parties, SF and DUP, are the dominant political parties within their respective communities. The fragmentation of the pro–GFA SDLP and the emergence of a resurgent SF was the result of the slow pace of change as well as SF's ability to harness the energy of grassroots politics within Catholic districts (Byrne 2007). In the past DUP politics was based on saying "No!" to political developments, as the DUP tried to slow the pace of change (Dixon 2007). However, moderate and extremist Unionism needed to do a deal before the demographic shift eventually unified the island's Catholics (McGarry and O'Leary 2007).

3. GEOGRAPHIC SPACE

Since stories encode cultural norms with regards to the relationship of people to their natural milieu (Senehi 2002), geographical places have cultural and symbolic significance for ethnic groups. Rival ethnic groups develop powerful ties to places over time that often end up in a zero-sum confrontation (Cunningham and Byrne 2006). Ethnic identity, different cultural worldviews, and geographic space become a part of a group's historical story, justifying territorial claims in we-they terms (Senehi 2002). Cultural signposts such as wall murals, footpaths painted with group colors, and national flags signify the territory of each community in NI (Byrne 2002). For example, tensions heighten in flashpoint neighborhoods such as the Lower Ormeau Road in Belfast and the Garvaghy Road in Portadown during the marching season. In the wake of a demographic shift in NI, the relative loss of a population majority increases insecurities within the Protestant community.

4. TIME

As the past and present are fused together in a "time collapse" (Volkan 1998), historical battles and myths and cultural events serve to illustrate the victimization or cultural superiority of each group. Ethnocultural institutions such as the Gaelic Athletic Association (GAA) or the Orange Order exclude members of the other community from participating in their activities. Since ethnic conflicts are often framed as being about past events that have disrupted interethnic relations (Senehi 2000), the fusion of memory and history is critical. Memories of past conflicts are passed intergenerationally through the storytelling process, claiming a glorious past that may be inaccurate or incomplete (Senehi and Byrne 2006). "Transcultural storytellers" who represent their community to others can break the cycle of destructive stories and build a shared identity (Senehi 2002).

5. SIEGE MENTALITY

Historically Loyalists and Unionists protected the British link to safeguard Protestant heritage and identity. With regard to the ambiguous

political status of NI as an integral part of the UK, Protestants were ultimately loyal to the queen rather than her government as the unending
symbol of their British identity (Byrne 1997). Protestant Unionists act
as a besieged community living in a perpetual state of insecurity, using
injustices of the past to legitimate and justify actions taken in the present
against the Catholic Nationalist community (Dixon 2000). For example,
Protestants point to the 1989 Remembrance Day bombing in Enniskillen
as an example of not trusting the Catholic community to give voice to the
traditional Unionist position of "No Surrender!" However, the absence
of the PIRA threat with its 1994 cease-fire stripped traditional Unionism
of its raison d'être to defend the Union between NI and Britain from its
Catholic enemies.

6. MALE PATRIOTS

In NI strong male patriots defend the ethnic homeland, while women and
children remain on the margins of political life (Mitchell 2006). Gender
differences are socially constructed in NI as the male warrior's courage
and roughness is idolized in the defense of the ethnic group (Mitchell
2006). During the Troubles women members of Loyalist and Republican
paramilitary groups acted as couriers and smuggled weapons, rarely taking part on the front line of fighting with the security forces.

6. Economic Factors

1. POPULISM

It has been argued that Catholics in Northern Ireland are 2.5 times
more likely than Protestants to be unemployed (Byrne and Irvin 2001).
The Unionist government carefully engineered a policy of anti-Catholic
discrimination in areas of housing and employment, forcing many to
emigrate so that the Catholic birth rate remained low (McGarry and
O'Leary 1995). However, Althusserian Marxists stress the internal dis-
unity between Populists and Anti-Populists of the Protestant bloc (Bew
et al. 1979, 1995). The state was founded in intense political instability.
Threats from Britain and the Republic of Ireland created the maximum
possible degree of Unionist unity. This meant an increasing reliance on
a police force—the RUC—and a Special Constabulary—the B Specials—
under local control and responsive to local Protestant pressures (Bew et
al. 1995). Thus, the role of British imperialism was minimized, and as
pointed out, between 1922–69, NI was largely ignored by Britain. The
McBride Principles, coupled with the 1975 Fair Employment Agency,
were put in place to prevent discriminatory practices in the workplace.

However, sectarianism as a practice continues in nonskilled and semi-skilled employment.

2. ECONOMIC POLICY

Whether or not it ignored NI from 1922 onward, Britain certainly financed the state and held ultimate sovereignty and responsibility (McGarry and O'Leary 1995, 2007). Whatever British government was in power, the state of NI was always the British state and is so to the present day. As far as NI is concerned then, there would seem to be many obstacles in the path to economic collaboration between both communities and socialism. Rose (1971) contends that Ireland is indeed no place for socialists or socialism. The fact that such contradictory theories—the anti-imperialist and Althusserian Marxist schools—have caused fundamental differences between socialists and led to a failure to construct a coherent and widely accepted policy for the advancement of socialism gives further credence to this argument. The fundamentally sectarian character of NI's political culture has obscured differences between right-wing and left-wing ideologies that mold party systems in other parts of Western Europe, including England. Normal left–right politics in NI can never take place while partition and the Anglo-Irish Treaty remain the primary issue for the electorate to vote on. On the other hand, the assertion that if Britain leaves NI, then normal politics can take over in a new thirty-two-county Republic may also appear shaky (Dixon 2007).

The aim of British economic policy in the late 1970s was to bring the Northern Irish economy into parity with the rest of the UK (Bew and Patterson 1985; Byrne and Irvin 2002). Massive infusions of capital were invested in NI that dealt with only the symptoms (security) and not the underlying causes (discrimination, poverty) of the economic situation (Bew et al. 1995). The result of economic policy was to increase unemployment, which led to greater structural inequalities between Protestants and Catholics, intensified polarization, and sustained sectarianism (O'Leary and McGarry 1993).

Bew and Patterson (1985) note that economic policies—a system of crisis management, a series of bungles, mistakes, and miscalculations to manipulate and domesticate, not to eradicate the problems—were only palliative and superficial in their effects. Capital was not poured into NI and not enough money was spent on housing. The British government had to appear to be doing something to get local politicians to support the Direct Rule regime (Bew and Patterson 1985). The policy of giving NI parity with the rest of the UK resulted in massive cutbacks in public spending, especially in education, and like the rest of the UK led to increased unemployment and polarization.

3. INTERNAL COLONIALISM

Since the core in London deliberately directed its economic policies and resources to peripheral areas in the Celtic fringe where members of its group were in the majority (Hechter 1975), internal colonialism ensured the nonequitable distribution of resources. Bew and Patterson (1985) contend that between 1969 and 1971, the British government introduced, first, a policy of neutralization that disbanded the B Specials and disarmed the RUC, and second, one of accommodation by reform of local government that replaced local authorities with district councils that had certain powers transferred from local to central control. These policies failed to accommodate Catholics into the NI state system because they failed to eradicate the material causes of Catholic discontent, such as unemployment and bad housing (Bew and Patterson 1985). For example, in the past, the level of unemployment west of the Bann in the predominantly Catholic areas of Derry, West Tyrone, and Fermanagh ensured a high level of unemployment within the Catholic community.

4. POVERTY AND POLITICAL VIOLENCE

Because it appealed to their sense of spirit, adventure, excitement, prestige, and grievance (Byrne 1995), during the Troubles impoverished, alienated, and unemployed working-class youth joined the burgeoning ranks of Republican and Loyalist paramilitary organizations. For example, in the wake of Bloody Sunday in 1973, young Catholics joined the PIRA en masse as they perceived no way out of their economic and political predicament. Moreover, as Whyte (1990) suggests, a "chill factor" impacts the economic climate since people won't work in a community dominated by the Other for fear of targeted assassinations by paramilitaries. Catholics also couldn't join the security forces because they were perceived as "legitimate targets" by the PIRA.

5. COLONIZER-COLONIZED RELATIONSHIP

The French colonizer in Algeria established a racist apparatus to justify, legitimate, and protect his economic privileges (Memmi 1974). The Algerian state had a strong police force to police the "wicked native," a government to rule the "backward and ignorant native," and a judicial system to punish the native (Memmi 1974). In Northern Ireland Unionist Populists sought to prevent a working-class alliance between Protestants and Catholics in order to preserve the economic power base of the Unionist economic elite. With the beginning of the Troubles in NI, the socioeconomic problem—that the main divisions in Ireland were between

Nationalism and Unionism and not labor and class—was pressed to the forefront of socialist thinking.

A wealth of new ideas about why socialism was so weak in Ireland developed, and a series of theories led to conflicts and divisions within socialist thinking, which, as a result, inhibited the growth of socialism. For example, anti-imperialist Marxists such as Eamonn McCann (1974) and Michael Farrell (1980, 1983) saw NI as an artificial creation established on the basis of an alliance forged between the Unionist bourgeoisie, who needed to retain the union to safeguard imperial markets, and the British ruling class, who wished to continue the occupation of NI for economic, political, and strategic reasons. British imperialism divided the working class in NI, and the constant British presence keeps the sterile question of Orange and Green alive. They argue that socialism in Ireland can only thrive once the struggle for national liberation is completed and the manipulation of the workers by the bourgeoisie ended.

6. DIASPORA

During the Troubles the Protestant and Catholic ethnic diaspora sent economic aid and munitions to support and resist the Republican armed struggle (Guelke 1988). As Adrian Guelke (1988) suggests, there was an international dimension to the conflict when outside forces became directly involved. For example, Northern Aid (NORAID) in the United States and Libya's Colonel Gaddafi supplied the PIRA with M14 rifles (the widow maker), AK47 assault rifles, Semtex explosives, and surface-to-air missiles. The SADF and Scottish Loyalists also supplied Loyalist paramilitaries with Kalashnikov assault rifles and explosives.

CONCLUSIONS

Most of the general public seems to be on board with the power-sharing deal made by Gerry Adams and Ian Paisley, who appear to be controlling hard-liner elements within their respective parties. The people of NI can struggle through a full term of the Belfast Assembly and then have elections at the end where they can judge the parties on their performance in government. The power-sharing deal will most probably stick partly because of the old adage that it takes the extreme parties to make an effective peace deal (Ryan 2007). The rejectionists that are left on each side are now too weak to bring down the GFA. Egotism and short-term political expediency are at work. However, some potential problems with the peace process might include:

(1) In the short term economic rather than political problems may be the biggest threat to the peace process as people are now used to the peace process being associated with an economic boom in NI. However, what will happen when, and if, the economy starts to decline?

(2) Who will replace Ian Paisley as leader of the DUP, and what impact will this have on the peace process?

(3) How will the Unionists react to SF's electoral ambitions in Eire? Can they cope with a situation where SF could hold the balance of power in the Oireachtas?

(4) Eventually, when they have the population numbers, SF will pursue the self-determination referendum stipulated in the GFA. If that happens, what occurs then? How will the powerful DUP react if such machinery as the sovereignty referenda agenda becomes a reality?

(5) The NI economy has a continuing and unsustainable dependence on the public sector for jobs and investment while a small and vulnerable private sector lacks the critical mass to create a level of wealth to grow the economy significantly in the face of global competition. How will a high level of unemployment within such a young workforce impact intergroup relations in the future?

(6) Can the spoilers, the RIRA and the Orange Defenders, take down the Belfast Assembly by ratcheting up the violence? The UVF just announced they will continue to seek peace but refuse to disarm any weapons. Meanwhile, a bomb in Co. Donegal was found in April 2007 and disarmed by the Gardaí, who attributed it to the RIRA.

Conflict is a dynamic and contradictory process that needs a holistic, theoretical framework to be correctly understood. This chapter used the social cubism analytical model to provide a comprehensive and holistic understanding of the various relationships that drive the NI conflict. Its conclusion must acknowledge the functional and sometimes essential role that conflict plays in assisting groups to protect their boundaries and identity. Conflict resolution interventionists and policy makers must understand the nature of both intergroup and intragroup conflict in escalating tension, rigidity, and hostility if effective conflict resolution mechanisms, economic aid, and political policies are to be introduced into that milieu.

3

Economic Development and Assistance in Peace Building: The Transformation of Postconflict Ethnopolitical Conflict

INTRODUCTION

DURING THE COLD WAR, POLICY MAKERS and scholars paid little attention to ethnic conflicts. This disregard for the importance of ethnic issues in world affairs was overtaken in stunning fashion, by recent events in Kosovo, Sudan, and Iraq among others. Scholarly research of protracted ethnopolitical conflicts in the former Soviet Union, former Yugoslavia, Africa, and the Middle East tend to take the perspective that these conflicts are taking place due to the collapse of authoritarian rule or the reconfiguration and fragmentation of the international system (Pearson 2001; Sandole 1999). Other analyses focus on the impact of ethnic nationalism on intergroup relations, the sharing of political and socioeconomic resources, the impact of democratization on intergroup relations, destructive stories and myths that demonize other ethnic groups, and the lack of state effectiveness in addressing the concerns of ethnic minorities (Byrne and Irvin 2000; Senehi 2000).

Recently the international community has adopted a wide range of strategies from peace enforcement to humanitarian intervention to de-escalate, manage, and settle a plethora of protracted ethnopolitical conflicts (Crocker et al. 2001). Since the end of the Cold War the international community has been striving to adopt a more conceptual, analytical, and systematic peace-building approach that identifies a number of critical actions and tracks to build a sustainable long-term peace (Lederach 1997). The complexity of conflict and cultural context necessitates a sensitive, coordinated, and integrated approach that combines security and demilitarization (disarmament), political transition (the protection of human rights, institutional reform, power-sharing governments, elections), development (economic rehabilitation, capacity building), and reconciliation and social rehabilitation (truth and reconciliation commissions, storytelling intervention processes) within every individual cultural context (Jeong 2005). Such a multitrack process that involves internal and external stakeholders must take place at the local community level as well as the national level within short, medium, and long-term time frames in order to empower the grass roots to achieve certain goals and to frame policies that work best in different circumstances (Byrne and Keashly 2000; Diamond and McDonald 1996).

In some cases successful third-party intervention by the international community may foster a peace-building process that engages ethnic groups to stay associated with each other under some part of an over-arching political framework such as ethnic elite power sharing (Leder-ach 1997). There is also recognition by the international community that intervention must involve a dynamic multidimensional peace-build-ing process that engages ethnopolitical groups to use economic develop-ment and assistance to tackle structural inequality as well as devising processes of reconciliation to heal from the traumatic past to restructure relationships positively (Byrne 2001b). This chapter explores the com-plementary roles of economic development, peace building and eco-nomic assistance, and transformational conflict resolution in reshaping divided societies.

ECONOMIC DEVELOPMENT AND ASSISTANCE: UNEQUAL AND UNEVEN DEVELOPMENT OF MODERNIZATION

There is no overarching grand theory of economic development. The field is so vast, the relevant literature so rich and diverse, and the prob-lem of obsolescent knowledge so rapid that it is difficult to present the theory of development (Grant and Nijman 1998). In the 1960s mod-ernization theorists argued that development was indeed a panacea to resolve and transform ethnopolitical conflicts. However, in response, dependency theorists such as Amin, Caradosa, Dos Santos, Escobar, Gunder Frank, and Wallerstein among others argued that development created a model of exploitation between the core and periphery in the global economy and would in fact exacerbate rather than ameliorate ethnopolitical conflicts.

Some dependency scholars contend that economic exploitation is an integral part of the capitalist system and is required to keep it function-ing, which results in a situation of dependency (Caradosa and Faletto 1979). The dependency process ensures that a certain number of coun-tries have their economies conditioned by the development and expan-sion of other core countries. This places the dependent or peripheral countries in a backward position, which enables the dominant countries to exploit them (Dos Santos 1970). Transnational class coalitions link comprador elites in the periphery with those in core-developed countries, and this class alliance works to the disadvantage of the working class in the periphery (Gunder Frank 1971). The comprador class introduces politico-economic policies that expand socioeconomic inequality, which takes the form of a wider rural-urban gap (Caradosa and Faletto 1979). Rural areas provide cheap labor and raw resources for the metropolis. Consequently, the relationship between both external and internal forces forms a complex whole whose structural links are rooted in the coincidence of interests between the comprador classes with foreign capitalists (Dos Santos 1970). Development benefits international banks and multinational corporations (MNCs) and increases socioeconomic inequalities between the classes at the periphery (Amin 1997).

Further, these dependency scholars argue that the mechanisms of dependency prevent peripheral countries from developing and contribute to worldwide uneven development. Capitalism is a system of monopolistic exchange that acts to transfer surplus value from peripheral areas to capitalist core centers (Jeong 2000). Development is restricted by the narrowness of markets, the balance of payment constraints, and technological dependence (Dos Santos 1970). Individuals, bureaucracies, and societies interact within the global context. We must understand the behavior that takes place within the structure of the global economy if we are to explain behavior within protracted ethnopolitical conflicts (Jeong 2005). Economic dependency explains the evolution and functioning of the world capitalist system that regulates peripheries (developing world) to subordinate positions within the global economy (Dos Santos 1970). Peripheral economies are thus distorted because of their economic dependence on the core metropolis (Gunder Frank 1971). Capitalism and its development throughout history work to the advantage of some states and to the detriment of others. For example, Wallerstein (1988, 2004) suggests that the division of labor in each society requires as well as increases inequality between regions. Thus, it is necessary to understand capitalism as a truly integrated world system to understand the fate of peripheral nations within the global economy and its impact on ethnopolitical conflicts (Agnew and Corbridge 1994).

Unequal development can also be found in industrial countries of the West. Hechter's (1975) internal colonialism theory suggests that the core (London) deliberately set out to impoverish peripheral groups and regions (Northern Ireland, Scotland, and Wales) within the Celtic fringe of Britain. The dialectical perspective of internal colonialism is a more adequate explanation of the persistence of ethnic attachments among peripheral groups in complex societies than theories that portray the periphery as culturally and structurally isolated from the core, stressing the relevance of dependency theory to the analyses of the internal structures of advanced societies.

According to Hechter (1975), the metropolis sets up a colonial structure that is reflected in the internal stratification of the periphery, where there will tend to be a dominant group oriented toward the core and a subordinate group with predominantly local orientations. Production in the periphery is subordinated to the needs of the core and peripheral areas are forced into a pattern of economic specialization and dependence. The cultural division of labor leads to the persistence of status group political orientations in the periphery and hence to what Hechter calls peripheral sectionalism. All actors, except the internal elite, unite behind the elements of a common regional culture and try to prevent the emergence of national solidarity throughout the state. This process results in an ethnically distinct economically disadvantaged peripheral population that mobilizes in reaction to the exploitation.

Thus, there must be a synergy between best development practices and a peace-building architecture to develop a better synergy of efforts to build sustainable peace in postconflict societies (Reychler and Paffenholz 2001).

Nexus Between Peace Building and Economic Development and Assistance

Ethnic nationalism is a mechanism for ethnic groups to belong, be recognized, and to seek revenge as they mobilize against the state (Smith 2003). Ethnically divisive strategies are chosen to provoke intrastate war (Carment and James 1997). Ethnic conflicts are driven by a plethora of interrelated issues that drive ethnic communities apart (Byrne and Carter 1996). Political elites devise destructive stories of past events to perpetuate new myths and group history that becomes enshrined in the collective memories of ethnic groups (Senehi 2002). External actors and events in the international system also impact the internal dynamics of ethnic conflicts since third parties can be both cause and cure of ethnic antagonisms (Byrne 2007).

Consequently, the international community has adopted a wide range of strategies to de-escalate and settle a number of ethnic conflicts (Pearson 2001; Sandole 2002). Humanitarian assistance, peacekeeping forces, and economic aid are employed to build the peace dividend in societies after violent conflict (Jeong 2005). For example, international nongovernmental organizations (INGOs) work to empower former child soldiers to heal and transition back to their communities while international funding agencies tackle social exclusion and economic deprivation (Byrne et al. 2006; Senehi and Byrne 2006).

In the aftermath of protracted ethnic conflict, the international community uses foreign aid as a peace-building mechanism (Carment and James 1997; Kaufman 2001) to address the root causes of ethnic conflict.

Economic intervention seeks to target socially excluded communities closely aligned with spoiler groups who can use violence to destabilize and destroy nascent peace processes (Darby and MacGinty 2000). Properly targeted foreign aid given toward the end of a protracted ethnic conflict could be an integral component of a postconflict peace-building process (Irvin and Byrne 2002). Research into the need to consolidate peace processes by economic means is relatively recent (Brynen 2000; Anderson 1999; Jeong 2005). The economic motivations leading to an escalation of ethnic violence, the links between economic aid and peace building, and economic recovery to restore peace have been comparatively neglected (Reychler and Paffenholz 2001). The findings on whether economic assistance can contribute to sustainable economic development, community empowerment, and reconciliation remain mixed (Byrne and Ayulo 1998; Byrne and Irvin 2001, 2002).

External foreign aid on its own is not a panacea to transform relationships into a culture of peace and may in fact be detrimental as group egotism shapes and reinforces rather than diminishes difference (Ryan 1996). Economic aid as part of a track in a multimodel and multilevel contingency intervention model involving a multiplicity of actors in a coordinated peace system is more effective in transforming conflict and building trust (Byrne and Keashly 2000). Such an organic intervention process builds new cooperative relationships through joint venture economic projects that promote contact at the local level and tackles structural inequalities coupled with problem-solving groups and storytelling interaction to cocreate new relationships and assist societies to recover from trauma (Senehi 2000, 2002). Lederach (1997) provides an analytical framework that taps into the indigenous culture's approach to create and sustain transformation and moves people toward restructuring relationships. Middle-tier elites play an important role in forging and sustaining the transformational peace system over time as they have significant connections both to the upper-tier elites and to the grass roots (Byrne 2001a; Lederach 1997).

Peace building is a long-term multidimensional process whereby people and context are given key resources to build sustainable peace (Lederach 1997). Citizens are encouraged to analyze critically, take action, and resolve their own problems (Freire 1999). Edward Schwerin (1995) defines grassroots citizen empowerment as being psychological (self-esteem and self-efficacy), social (developing new knowledge and skills), and political (participation and action) connecting the individual to the macro institutions of society. Grassroots empowerment or "people power" promotes a participatory democracy or power with "political process" that transforms conflict into a sustainable long-term peace (Woolpert, Slaton, and Schwerin 1998).

Grassroots empowerment is acknowledged by funding agencies as a critical component in the transformation of conflict (Jeong 2005). Discussing the potential of humanitarian assistance to influence the wider dynamics of peace and conflict, Goodhand and Atkinson (2001) make the point that donors need to be fully aware of the trade-offs and tensions that arise when pursuing multiple objectives that include peace, justice, and humanitarian needs. Donors must be transparent when exploring different objectives to arrive at an optimum policy (Goodhand and Atkinson 2001, 40).

Aid can complement a coordinated political process. Security and development must be mutually reinforcing because many of the threats that impact the international community arise largely from the failures of development (Tschirgi 2003, 13). Development cooperation, therefore, may need to integrate the following principles into an action agenda plan:

> Maximize indigenous ownership and participation, minimize dependency, reduce the dangers of violent conflict, work for the respect of human rights, preserve an even-handed commitment to development values and goals, strengthen coordination and coherence with other external actors, improve responsiveness and flexibility, listen and learn about specific country situations, promote more development-friendly policies and practices beyond traditional development assistance, and avoid making promises of aid that cannot be delivered or sustained. (Wood 2001, 53–54)

In the past, economic development focused on technology transfer rather than democracy and peace building (Jeong 2005). Today, the World Bank and the International Monetary Fund (IMF) tie aid packages to democratic values and liberal economic reforms (Grant and Nijman 1998). The belief held by some policy makers and scholars is that a vigorously expanding economy can mitigate and build peace in protracted ethnopolitical conflicts (Anderson 1999). Others are of the view that economic assistance must be an integral overall strategy of political accommodation and elite power sharing or efforts by external donors may cause harm (Esman 1997; McGarry and O'Leary 1995). The international donor community recognizes that building a sustainable economic infrastructure to create growth and employment needs to be in parallel with a multitrack peace-building process (Byrne and Irvin 2001, 2002).

International donor agencies and governments are now wary of simply providing economic assistance to transform deep-rooted conflict. A long-term approach to peace building necessitates the development of an interdependent web of partners for peace. Lederach (1997) argues that an organic peace-building model involves forging new ways of thinking about the waves of activity and how they relate to the overall context to create a framework for responsibility and accountability for the implications of the actions and to create a strategic commitment to maximize the proactive ingredients of a peace-building process (90).

Economic aid can also consolidate the peace process by addressing deep subjective issues (fear, misperceptions, and prejudice) by bringing people together through joint-venture projects, providing a critical space where they can get to know each other (Lederach 1997). Contact allows people to challenge stereotypes, empirically build trust, and restructure relationships around superordinate goals. Economic development cooperation can, in turn, spill over into political and cultural spaces. In the past, ethnic nationalism and myths, stereotyping, and exclusion from socioeconomic and political resources have served the interests of elites to polarize and escalate animosity between groups (Byrne and Irvin 2000). Thus, the peace-building process is comprised of interdependent roles, activities, and functions needed to build a sustainable peace process over the long term (Lederach 1995), which deals with structural inequality and economic deprivation as well as restructuring relationships.

The anticipated peace dividend must target excluded groups who have the arsenal and firepower to destroy a nascent peace process (Byrne 1995). The $2 billion in economic assistance to the Palestinian Authority (PA), for example, consolidated the Oslo peace process, shaping economic and political policies to combat poverty and promote community welfare and sustainable development (Brynen 2000, 2005). The peace dividend, therefore, involves all the stakeholders in a process that strengthens shared needs in a pattern of constructive interaction and that addresses structural inequalities to forge a peace culture built around a mutually beneficial relationship (Fitzduff 1996). Thus, the rehabilitation of societies coming out of protracted conflict involves a redefinition of social and ethnic groups to promote reconciliation and psychosocial healing and reconciliation as well as the transformation of economic policies and institutions in the public and private sector (Varynen 1997, 156).

However, the politics of economic aid too often reinforce rather than reduce blocks among ethnic groups (Anderson 1999). Economic aid may in fact be a weak tool in influencing the relationship between rival ethnic groups and in changing perceptions and behaviors (Byrne and Ayulo 1998). Economic assistance from international donor agencies without political complementarity and coordination is not a panacea to transform relationships (Esman 1997). An inclusive multitrack approach recognizing the multiplicity of actors and issues is a more appropriate strategy to transform relationships and build a structure that is sustainable (Byrne and Keashly 2000).

INGOs, NGOs, and international agencies are integrating new innovative peace-building initiatives into their humanitarian relief and development work, promoting nonviolent peace building in the process (Anderson 1999). In particular these organizations are flexible, efficient, and participatory in nature, building local capacity to secure a healthy society and a sustainable peace that empowers the local population (Junne and Verkoren 2004; Peck 1998). These organizations can also assist in analyzing and advocating policies that support socially disadvantaged groups, promote cross-community contact, and ecological and economic sustainability to address and transform the personal, relational, structural, and cultural dimensions and dynamics of conflict (Lederach 1997; Paffenholz and Reychler 2005).

The peace-building process also includes reconciliation built on a foundation of truth, mercy, justice, and peace that allows conflicting parties to develop new relationships based on apology, forgiveness, and trust in a process of truth telling (Lederach 1997; Senehi and Byrne 2006; Senehi 1996, 2000). In addition, international economic assistance as a track in the same peace-building process must tackle the causes of poverty and disadvantage that prevent human development and growth within the micro-, meso-, exo-, and macrosystems in order to forge an infrastructure to achieve and sustain conditions for peace and justice (Brynen 2000, 2005). Such a long-term peace-building process of roles and functions aims to build human and environmental security, social justice, sustainable development, human rights, democratic government, the rule of law, and cross-cutting confidence building measures that empower civil society.

TRANSFORMATIONAL CONFLICT RESOLUTION AND PEACE BUILDING

Transformational conflict resolution involves "the peace concepts, methods, norms, parties, practices, and processes that ethnic communities together use to transform underlying structural issues in the process of post-conflict peacebuilding" (Byrne 2001b, 4). Transformational conflict resolution (TCR) focuses on the what, how, where, and who of transforming structures, institutions, relationships, and political and socioeconomic issues to forge a culture of peace (Botes 2003). Three TCR models are outlined to illustrate critical components of the transformational peace-building process.

Galtung's Model

Galtung (1990, 1996) argues that violence is direct (an event), structural (a process or system of injustice), and cultural (a permanence such as art, language, ideology, religion, empirical, and formal science). Consequently, violence must be transformed by the grass roots into a sustainable peace-building process for positive as opposed to negative peace (the absence of war) to prevail. Peace building ensures the creation of a structural and cultural peace process as third parties identify the nonarticulated structural conflicts within the society and try to resolve them. This is a critical step on the pathway to a positive transformation of the conflict (Galtung 1996, 271).

Further, Galtung (1996), Paulo Freire (1999), and John Paul Lederach (1995) contend that the grass roots must be empowered to look within their own knowledge systems to critically analyze the root causes of conflict to transform cultural systems and structural processes in a multidimensional intervention to rebuild the civic culture. Elite politics on its own cannot build a sustainable peace. An elite solution in the form of a negotiated and signed document by the group leaders outlining the new political framework does not resolve all of the conflict (Galtung 1996, 89).

Lederach's Model

Peace building involves a coordinated relationship between grass roots, middle, and top leadership in a process that integrates a multiplicity of approaches to peace building—from prejudice reduction, to problem-solving workshops, to formal political negotiations (Lederach 1997). Sustainable peace building must take into account vertical and horizontal leadership to build capacity and to coordinate multilevel intervention and complementarity (ibid.). Human and collective security, social justice, and human rights must be addressed by transforming socioeconomic and political structures to nurture participatory democracy to build and sustain the peace process over the long term (ibid.).

Further, Lederach's (1995) belief in indigenous empowerment indicates that a sustainable empowerment suggests that the people within the conflict milieu must forge a sustainable peace process and structure. People's knowledge, understanding, and meaning of the conflict is socially constructed by their lived experience and informs how they process and respond to the conflict—constructively or destructively (ibid.). Relationships within the personal, cultural, and structural context are critical to transforming conflict nonviolently to sustain peaceful and respectful relationships at all levels embedded in the overall peace process (Lederach 1997). Reconciliation must include elements of truth, justice, mercy, and peace if a sustainable peace is to be maintained over time (ibid.). A process that articulates the interests and human needs of all members of society necessitate socioeconomic and political transformation of structures.

Innovation is necessary to build new relationships among different groups within society. An important meeting point between innovation and realism is reconciliation (Lederach 1997). Reconciliation is not pursued by minimizing the conflicting groups' affiliations; instead it is built on mechanisms that engage those in conflict with each other in human relationships. For example, Initiative 92, an independent citizens' group, was instituted to examine the ways for the conflict in Northern Ireland to cease, and for the communities to live together in peace (Pollack 1993). Six dialogue sessions were held with both communities; many interviews were conducted and the Opsahl Commission examined hundreds of written documents (Byrne 1995). The Opsahl Commission laid the groundwork for citizen empowerment and recognition that is built into the 1998 Good Friday Agreement (GFA).

Burton and Redekop's Model

John Burton (1987, 1990) argued that deep-rooted conflicts could be resolved by addressing threats to basic human needs. Burton (1990) defined basic human needs in terms of meaning, action, recognition, security, and connectedness that when self or group is threatened translate into structures of violence. Only with the fulfillment of basic human needs will conflict de-escalate and be resolved.

Vern Redekop (2002) develops Burton's analytical framework with René Girard's idea of mimetic violence (scapegoating) to understand how deep-rooted conflict and violence can be transformed into peace and reconciliation. Redekop contends that each of Burton's human needs incorporates a number of sub-needs that must be satisfied. For example, the elements of such a human needs structure would include meaning with sub-needs of insight, root metaphors, justice, paradigm, and world of meaning while action comprises the sub-needs of control of environment, power, autonomy, and agency. In addition, the need recognition is made up of the sub-needs of acknowledgment, appreciation, significance, dignity as self-worth, and saving face, while security encapsulates the sub-needs of welfare needs, human rights, physical, emotional, spiritual, and economic. Moreover, connectedness includes the sub-needs of belonging, community, language, tribe, land, and nature, and being/self comprises of the sub-needs of selfness, presence, character, heart, and emotions (ibid.). Thus, the conflict parties, third-party intermediaries, donors, and policy makers need to build the following framework into their peace-building process and structure.

When basic human needs are satisfied, self-recognizance replaces anger (meaning), self-esteem replaces depression (action), self-actualization replaces shame (recognition), self-confidence replaces fear (security), and self-respect replaces sadness (connectedness) (Redekop 2002). Thus, the dynamics of basic human needs grow, change, and face challenges through time in an ongoing interaction between people within a particular cultural context (ibid.).

Basic human needs embedded within a relational system must be acknowledged and incorporated into the peace-building process if individuals within groups are to be truly empowered and cultural and structurally violent institutions transformed into peaceful ones.

CONCLUSIONS

The growing interdependence, globalization, and fragmentation of world society are both natural and inevitable. One of the key factors contributing to rapid social change, and that manifests itself in the form of ethnic conflict, is the globalization and penetration of the macroeconomy in society. The expansion of advanced forms of communication and a growing interdependence among transnational actors has made the state increasingly obsolete and dysfunctional (Agnew and Corbridge 1994). As a result, ethnic conflicts can be explained, in part, by the institutional isolation of ethnic minorities from the rapidly developing global market of international society. Internally ethnic claims are made not only for the sake of group belonging but also for more socioeconomic inclusion.

Thus, providing institutional outlets for ethnic mobility may be one important pathway to address the ethnic stratification of international society that is fomenting ethnopolitical conflicts (Scott 1998). External donor agencies can tackle the structural sources of conflict by addressing socioeconomic underdevelopment as well as ethnocultural claims through reconciliation that contribute to protracted ethnopolitical conflicts. A comprehensive approach can move toward the allocation and redistribution of political and socioeconomic resources within the state.

4

Economic Assistance and People's Perceptions of Economic Development and Community Capacity Building

INTRODUCTION

EXTERNAL ECONOMIC FUNDING AGENCIES SEEK to facilitate an approach that helps communities assume responsibility for their growth and change and for shaping their own future (Curle 1990). Monies are to be used to stimulate the self-confidence of both Protestant and Catholic communities in NI, and to encourage the development of faith in their ability to recognize and then meet their own human needs (Byrne and Irvin 2000, 2002). Genuine community capacity building is coupled, therefore, with an unlimited capacity for achievement and the development of interdependent relations with others. This chapter analyzes the perceptions respondents had toward the role of the IFI and EU Peace and Reconciliation or Peace I funding agencies in community regeneration and community capacity building within NI.

The goal of economic development is to develop people's potentialities and to transform society (Galtung 1996). An engaged community of individuals can create and maintain the socioeconomic and political structures and material conditions that provide lasting satisfaction to their members and assist in transforming the social structure (Curle 1990; Galtung 1996). The central values and concepts within a process of transformational politics should also include: "(1) the personal empowerment of individual citizens; (2) grassroots direct democracy; (3) deep ecology, or an awareness and sensitivity to the interdependence of humankind and all aspects of its environment within the Earth's ecosphere; (4) respect, if not appreciation for, the vast diversity of races, sexes and lifestyles within any society and/or around the globe; (5) collaboration and co-operation being a superior way of human interaction to that of competitiveness" (Schwerin 1995, 5).

Transformational politics ensures hope and social justice that eliminates economic inequality within society as well as a process of healing that respects difference and promotes community, enhancing the optimal development of each human being's potential (Schwerin 1995; Woolpert, Slaton, and Schwerin 1998). Contact plus confidence-building measures, sustainable economic assistance, and economic regeneration are critical ingredients of peace building (Love 1995). Economic development must be a part of any peace-building process and must contain the values of dignity, equality, freedom, justice, and respect within its philosophical framework (Curle 1990). For those reasons, the role of the IFI and the EU Peace I Fund is to impact socioeconomic structural problems, socially and economically, as part of an overall intervention strategy to build sustainable peace and postconflict reconstruction in NI.

However, structural problems contributed to the outbreak of the Troubles in 1969 and were exacerbated by the political violence that rocked NI for more than thirty years. Toward the end of the 1960s, the internal cultural division of labor, in part, was critical to the ethnoreligious mobilization of the Nationalist community in NI (Whyte 1990). The metropolis in the core allowed the economic metropole in Belfast to create structural conditions that led to segmentation and hierarchy within NI's economy (Bew et al. 1979, 1995). The Populist policies of the NI state that manufactured discrimination in housing, employment, and job creation worked to the advantage of the Unionists and to the disadvantage of the Nationalist community. The unequal distribution of economic resources was one of the "Six Points" that the NI Civil Rights Association petitioned for in 1968 to reform the state and make it less sectarian (Byrne 1997). Persistent economic inequalities were not the only reason for the mobilization of the Catholic community in 1968 and the countermobilizations of the Protestant community as other political factors were also evident (Irvin 1999). However, the economic marginalization of the Catholic working-class community has always played an important role in the momentum of Nationalist opposition to the British government.

Thus, external economic funding can be used as a political mechanism to respond to ethnopolitical strife (Esman 1997). Within the context of NI, economic resources were not used in the past by the British government to placate or mollify the working classes who have traditionally provided the cannon fodder for the rival paramilitary groups (Bew et al. 1979, 1995; Irvin 1999). Indeed, the economic policies of the British government sustained sectarianism by creating structural inequalities between Unionists and Nationalists (Bew et al. 1979; O'Leary and McGarry 1993). Moreover, Provisional Irish Republican Army car bombs used to cripple the economy, and the intransigence and aloofness of British economic policy have worked together to make NI one of the poorest economic regions within the UK and within the EU (Boyle and Hadden 1994; Byrne 2001a). Yet NI is not like any other region within the UK or the EU. Political violence has racked the region for more than thirty years and has stripped away any vestiges of a once-vibrant economy.

Massive cutbacks in public spending by the British government in the past have increased unemployment, especially in traditionally working-class Catholic urban areas in Belfast and Derry (Dixon 2000; Gaffkin and Morrissey 1990). Marginalization, in turn, increased discontent and estrangement and deeply entrenched the feeling of living in a bicommunal society within both communities (Cunningham 1994; McGarry and O'Leary 1995). The British government addressed the symptoms by reacting to the deteriorating economic situation in NI rather than design realistic economic policies to treat the deep-rooted causes of the problem (Bew and Patterson 1985).

However, in the 1990s, NI's business community recognized that a peace process would stimulate economic growth, which would in turn consolidate peace (Friedman and Killick 1999, cited in Buchanan 2005, 47). The business track of a multitrack intervention system was comprised of a policy arm that authored the peace dividend paper and a lobby arm through the Group of Seven. In 1996, the Group of Seven consulted with NI's political parties on the economic rationale for peace. In collaboration with the Community Relations Council, the Group of Seven created antisectarian policies to protect NI's workers from harassment and discrimination. The Group of Seven emphasized that NI had to choose between "peace, progress, and prosperity and a future as one of the world's trouble spots. The group recognizes that business cannot build peace alone . . . but [its] efforts made it less easy for the parties to simply walk away" (Friedman and Killick 1999, 2, cited in Buchanan 2005, 47).

Externally, the U.S. corporate sector successfully played a role in 1984 in creating the MacBride Principles for U.S. businesses operating in NI that addressed human rights and justice issues in the workplace (Guelke 1988). In addition, the IFI was created in 1986 with Australia, Canada, the EU, New Zealand, and the United States as primary donor countries, forging an economic development incentive to stimulate employment and growth as a mechanism to foster peace and reconciliation in NI (ibid.). Similar track two interventions by the EU Peace I Fund also highlighted the role of economic assistance in targeting socioeconomic needs, relational reconciliation, grassroots empowerment, and sustainable economic development (Byrne and Ayulo 1998; Irvin and Byrne 2002).

The respondents presented below express recurrent themes to explain the role of the funding process in economic regeneration and community capacity building in both NI and the border counties. These themes evolved from a sequence of questions based on the participants' understanding of economic development and politics in their everyday lives. Respondents hold mixed views regarding the role of economic aid in developing and empowering local communities.

Economic Regeneration and Community Development

Northern Ireland is an underdeveloped periphery on the peripheral fringe of both the EU and the UK. Instances of discrimination in employment, housing, and regional policy have been well documented as having led to sectarianism within a bicommunal society (Bew et al. 1995). Similarly, the border is an underdeveloped area within the Republic of Ireland. The Troubles spilled over and devastated the economic infrastructure of many border communities.

Some of the civil servants in Dublin who administer the IFI and the EU Peace I Fund believe that the economic aid is impacting the development of local community economies. A senior Dublin civil servant suggests that local communities know what is in their own interests. He is of the opinion that it is important to include a diversity of people in local projects so that ownership is not with one or two people. He adds that both the IFI and the EU Peace I Fund has empowered local people to own the process rather than central government. In addition, he argues that it is critical that the aid goes directly to community projects:

> The Rowntree Report, supposed impartial, was very unfair in its criticisms and missed the point on very many areas that there had been a deliberate attempt to distance central government from the implementation of the program now, and because it was seen as being important to the success of the program on the ground to show that there was no mucking around with money, and to show that there was no way that we were using peace money to fund things that otherwise would have been done under other enterprise programs and so on.

Another senior Dublin civil servant suggests that development officers are in constant communication with each other over community group projects, especially if they perceive that a certain project might be better funded by another agency:

> It sounds marvelous to talk about coordination, but every time that Mr. X, the interreg development officer, goes out for a cup of coffee in Monaghan, he either ends up meeting people from the Peace Administration or IFI or the lay staff who in turn would be in contact with cross-border groups. And, similarly, anytime I would have a meeting with someone from the other government departments, I would hear something about the peace programs. It is a very, very small world out there and we have pro forma structures and yet spend large amounts of money and design for much larger areas of the public.

He adds:

Yes, I'm on the Southern side. Some people mention faces like long-haired mandarins from Dublin coming down here to tell us what to do. I mean, you had that because you had at the local level, you had very well-developed local authority structures and systems and county enterprise development people, and they were doing a lot and they were tied in locally, and politicians are close to them. You also have county councillors who are nervous of the voluntary sector, and there didn't seem to be the same political necessity for it down the South as there might have been in the North. So I would say there was a learning phase in the early stages of the Peace and Reconciliation Program at this level between the NGOs involved, ADM [Area Development Management], Combat Poverty, and the government structures, probably more local government structures. And I'd say both sides had a certain amount to learn. My understanding is that cooperation now is quite good, and some of the initial hiccups have been essentially overcome and there is good cooperation. What you have up there, you have funds and privileges, if you like, [that] are being distributed by an NGO, at an NGO level. Whereas you have structures that have political clout that haven't got the access to those funds, and you obviously are going to get a certain amount of tension in the initial stages, and I'm not surprised there was some initial concern. I think that the NGOs are making very good coordination with the local agencies because that suits them for the quality of projects as well. And the local agencies realize that this is a reality they have there, so they may as well try and direct these funds as best they can.

Development consultants assist local communities with their proposals, but not all applications are funded. The consultants nurture the project along but do not try to control it. The IFI has to carefully monitor each project to account for the spending of funds to the donors. Here is another Dublin civil servant's picturesque description of the IFI process:

IFI looks not only for a project that is professional, or from a technical point of view hangs together, but also corresponds to real need in the community. People can want to do things, but it will not really correspond to need. For instance, a lot of communities feel a community hall is a great thing. When you really sit back and analyze it, what does it really do by way of long-term employment or by way of bringing money into the community or by way of bringing activity? It gives a "feel good" factor to the community, but perhaps it is weak on the economic regeneration side, so we have tried to work with the communities again going back to what I was saying. So a community can come at any stage of development, but perhaps it is weak on the economic regeneration side, so we have tried to work with it. It may be somewhere here beginning to articulate some kind of self-identity really, which it does not know, or maybe it is very far along here and has its identity together, got an economic plan together or got everything together, and some communities will. Often it comes with one or two people, if they are particularly dynamic, who might come with a project made almost like X, which was a very quick project from our point of view, it was almost made. Even with that sometimes, you find that the dynamism often is not enough to articulate a project economically, and that is where some kind of professional help may be needed. When we can, our development consultant will do that, and for instance, Mr. X in Sligo is working with the North Side Community Partnership. He did this with the local community and helped them with these cash flow charts, and a chart that showed the source of funding and all that sort of thing, and where we can, we would do that, but that is not always possible. So we would try to keep that kind of expenditure to a minimum where it has to occur. We would try to ensure that the community group gets good value for money, and we would usually work through our development consultant in recommending not a particular, but at least a choice of people to the community because there is a fine line which we do not want to cross either—where you are directing the community so that they are not really doing their project. So you are trying to advise and nurture it along so that in a way they are still responsible for it and the running of it and feel that it is their own and corresponds to the basic needs of the community. . . . If you do a project, which, number one, is not properly thought out and corresponding to a need, and, number two, is not properly put together, then the other side of it is that our donors come back and say, "What kind of crazy projects are you doing? This thing does not hang together and moreover it does not correspond with needs on the ground." So that it is a kind of squeeze we are operating into, and we need the reassurance of what we are doing is right or at least it is on the right road and the strategic plan will often open the gate on that road, and when you come to here you will need to tie it down in such a way that it hangs together economically.

In addition, a Dublin civil servant highlights that the IFI is more flexible than the EU Peace I Fund in its approach to distributing funds. He suggests that the IFI's broader approach makes it extremely attractive to applicants in comparison to trying to access Peace I money out of local county councils:

Why not get the Republicans of Cork dealing with whoever is in the North? And they probably need to deal with them actually. Dundalk people now feel differently and Newry-Mourne people now feel differently, and Belfast people and Dundalk people now feel differently. Like those way down in West Cork and Kerry, which is a fairly big Nationalist area as it stands anyway. They are not involved in that processing in some senses and maybe they should be. Maybe the business community down there should be. There are some activities under IFI that have worked, like the health care group. The Southern health care companies have worked with the North under IFI under our business development program on the basis that it helped companies in the North. You know, saying we have plenty of interpretation for this, for the benefit of companies in the North. IFI have taken a broader approach whereas the others are less likely to do it on the basis of upsetting the applecart and stuff. I would think that it would make a lot of sense for one of those programs to take an all-Ireland view. I don't think it's going to be too easy to get the ones that have relationships between North–South industries or government departments come into view on it, to do it as easily.

In addition, a community development officer with the EU Peace I Fund in Co. Monaghan suggests that EU development officers on the Irish Republic side of the border know the basic human needs of local people with whom they work closely on the ground. With the ongoing paramilitary cease-fires, there is optimism from alienated border communities that political and economic change is possible. He believes that economic assistance is psychologically empowering local marginalized communities:

Think of the language we have lived here with. It was a language of exclusion. It was a language of marginalization. It was a language of peripherality, and therefore it was a cause of conflict. I think that what we have seen, to me, since even that first cease-fire, is that maybe there is that little change. There is that thing . . . that people are beginning to talk about a future. There is a little bit of optimism. I think that we are seeing a little bit more investment. And I think the word hope—and I remember there was a candidate running in the United States, was it Jesse Jackson?—who used to say, "keep hope alive." . . . And that in the border counties that was what an awful lot of smaller voluntary sector community groups were doing. They were trying to keep hope alive. In a sense they were being beaten back all of the time by a system or a hierarchy or impediments to be able to change things.

In addition, an EU Peace I officer from Co. Tyrone's dynamic and colorful description of the funding process illustrates that those applicants who have personal contact with the funding agencies know when to apply for the grants:

I think European funding agencies think that if they advertise in the paper that packages are open from April 1 to September 2, that is sufficient. They go around, and they will do a couple of say, six meetings, put an ad in the paper and the people who turn up are the people who know about it anyways nine times out of ten. I think that what you need to do is to take a step further. What that is I am not quite sure, but you know that is for making public awareness of the funding. The classic one was

Peace and Reconciliation funding. I mean, target it in areas where there was [the] most trouble. And it is given to farmers who were developing pseudo-environmental improvements in their farms. It opened at 9:00 AM and closed at 12:00 noon for one day. It was called FACES. I don't know what it stands for. It was a classic example of not getting knowledge of it out. There was a whole furor about it, and, I mean, that is going back a few years. The papers were full of it. Everybody was complaining from an agricultural point of view, and what in reality actually happened was the big farmers, dairy farmers, big landowners, they had it sussed months ago. They knew when to apply. They knew when it was going to open and they probably knew it was going to close at 5:00 or 8:00 PM. And the applications went in, and the normal small-time farmers firstly opened for only one day. They said because of the deluge of applications. Once again, why was there a deluge of applications if only certain people knew about it, whatever mechanism within? I don't know . . . so that is a working example of the problem.

Further, he emphasizes that new community groups do not know that the funding agencies exist. This is particularly so for inexperienced, rural groups who are trying to find their feet. Also, he suggests that the IFI has been around for the past nineteen years so that people are very aware of its presence in the community, in contrast to the EU Peace I Fund, which is quite new. Of the IFI he says:

The first problem for a lot of groups is actually knowing the background, the fundamental problem, knowing that the funding exists in the first place. Not so much with IFI, because the IFI more or less has been there before. It has been floating around for a while [but applying for European financial advantages is a new phenomenon]. Groups may be aware of the main European funding flares, [such as] the likes of Peace and Reconciliation, one of the main European funding sources that people would know. In terms of rural development, it is just rural development that I am involved with. European funding can be exceedingly complicated in terms of the numbers accessing funding, which is available stretching from . . . there is general rural development, which is under a LEADER 2 package. There is also funding, various types of funding through the Department of Agriculture. . . . The other big problem is that organizations are community groups that are up and running for say five or ten years. Obviously by mentioning the fact of their experience and of any training they have possibly done from IFI is an advantage, who have their ears to the ground. And probably nine times out of ten they will analyze who gets funding in terms of community groups up and running for a long time, and in many ways they are not probably the group you should be focusing on. You should be focusing on the one group that are newly born and kind of finding their feet looking at what low-level, medium-level-type projects they could become involved with.

A consultant with the IFI in the border area expresses a positive attitude toward IFI consultants who get out into the communities in the border area and meet local people on the ground. He also suggests that if a community project is very complex, it will need a lot of direction from the IFI consultant.

Sometimes they will get consultants. Usually they will get a consultant to help them, and that is a whole area of danger as well—that consultants can come in, maybe consultants who are used to dealing with normal private business, and they can take over and very often be seen to drive the project as opposed to serving the needs of the community and the interests of the community. . . . We would often sit down with them and help them to compile the relevant information and to clarify their objectives, so that they can put together a coherent proposal. But there are a growing number of consultancy firms out there who are good in dealing with communities and who do have the sensitivities that are required to deal with the community, where very often you are dealing with voluntary people giving up voluntarily of their time as opposed to being full-time professionals. . . . There are certain projects that need to be driven by a consultant. They need to be driven from on top almost. Where particularly the more complex broadly based projects like I mentioned to you about a proposal for a cycle way based on the old railways that is not in the exclusive ownership of any local authority or any particular individual, something is quite widespread throughout the whole Northwestern region. No one individual is going to be able to drive that. For example, Leitrim County Council was to take the initiative on that. They would find it extremely difficult to bring along the other relevant authorities. Whereas, if somebody without any personal agenda comes into the situation and points out the issues very pragmatically, very objectively, the potential benefits that it could recruit from the development of this resource, there is a much better likelihood of the necessary authorities coming in behind it rather than it been driven by one particular sectoral or geographic interest. So in some cases, yes, projects do need to be driven a bit from outside or from above, but there must always be an exit mechanism. There must always be a point where that person gets off.

District partnerships have helped local communities by setting up local structures to provide social inclusion in Derry. A project officer with Derry District Partnerships indicates her support of the district partnership format. She goes on to say:

I think first of all that I would definitely keep the district partnerships, and that is not because I am working in one. They have been the vehicle by which you could actually see that a couple of the agencies and that money have been caught up in their own agendas and nobody is ever too sure if they had applied, if it is something they would have got anyway or is it in addition to what they would have got? I think that within the structures, we and the themes that we have, that it was great to have that, but we see that there was so much competition here that there was other projects that we would have loved to have funded, and I think that we should work on that. I think we should keep the structures that we have, and those that we have are great, urban, rural, social inclusion. Let's take them forward and even look at projects that have developed over a few years. But now they could reach a much wider market and put a much wider impact if we give them another injection of money and to take it that wee bit forward. I think that you would be very reliant on the people on the Forum this minute and take their experiences and try not to reinvent the wheel and start over again. You look to see what has worked and you help to develop those structures. We also take into consideration what would happen in the external environment. You know people move on, can structures still be in place without the people who were there in the beginning?

In addition, a community group leader in Derry is of the opinion that economic commitment and community involvement are critical ingredients for the rebuilding of the societal framework within NI. The district partnerships can work in concert with the community to create employment in the city that enhances the self-esteem, self-worth, and self-efficacy of each citizen to build a better society for everyone in NI:

In pure economic terms, of course, you can't ever argue against money coming, investment coming, creating long-term work. You really can't argue against that absolutely. As long as it is linked into a local strategy and the partnership models, which are now coming from Europe, are part of that where you marry statutory economic policy to the community. The community is now validly staying as a social partner. In NI, I think there has to be a continued mix of sheer hard economic good investment—sheer hard job creation along with this horrible cliché term, "capacity building," for local people to build away and work away. But this bottom line that could tell how many jobs were created isn't always the best material on which to value it as community development profit, because a process itself is a long, slow process. Confidence-building measures for the long term and that it's not going to culminate in a job next week. It's about much, much more than that—economic development, economic investment, economic interests. People work with dignity with a pound in their pocket. They become participatory by the very active economy. They become better citizens.

In contrast, a community leader in Co. Monaghan believes that local community groups feel isolated from both local authorities and central government. Moreover, these communities are caught between the rivalries of funding agencies, local grassroots organizations, as well as local and central governments that are vying to distribute the funds.

And by far the biggest problem is the people who need help both at the unemployed level and communities who have lost confidence by and large, and this is a big problem. They have lost confidence with statutory agencies and rightly so because they don't care about them. Nor do the politicians, because there are no worthwhile votes in the area, so we are not politically important.

Implicit in a community group leader from Co. Monaghan's story is the view that Peace I funding is too complicated for local community groups to tap into. Clearly, he believes that the contact between agency consultants and the community makes the IFI process easier to apply to. He suggests that local community groups do not have the sophistication needed to tackle the EU Peace I application package because it is less clear compared to the IFI application process:

> The development officers will be canonized as saints sometime . . . both the two people that operate here . . . both Mr. X across the border and Mr. Y on this side. European funding is too complicated and too bureaucratic for community groups. You want to be very high-powered. We are quite familiar with the programs and they are well enough advertised and that, if you want to know where to look for them. Not sure about the ordinary person on the ground, but for the fact that we are an information center, we would be fairly well up to speed. . . . There is a chap called Mr. Z at European Information Point. Any information we want to get we would get it from him within a day or so. But sometimes we haven't got the expertise to know what to do with it. We are not high-powered to tap into them. We look at them and we are just like the hawks looking into the orchard and the birds do hide from them. We just haven't the power in ourselves yet to be able to go for these things.

If there is any lingering ambiguity about whether his feeling toward the IFI consultants is positive, there is no doubt when he continues to support the consultants' work in his story. Here are his further remarks on this point:

> First of all, the IFI is promoted widely on the ground, and we are very familiar with it, and it would have excellent officers that would be local development officers with them. It was probably the IFI officer, Mr. Y, in this area that got our group up and running as a community umbrella group, bringing all the factions of the community together and organizing them into modular training. We would be quite well aware of the IFI program. We were able to accept money from it for a feasibility study on that workhouse building. They paid approximately 75 percent of the cost of the feasibility study, which was working out at around £12,000, and we were awarded £9,000. Basically, they gave us the initial leg-up to be able to get it together to develop a strategic plan for the area. So we would

have done this modular training that they encouraged us to do with FAS, which is a national training agency. We did four years' training of modular training, which is eleven sessions with a facilitator. Then in between those sessions, we had to do our homework. . . . Certainly, the IFI has made a huge impact on the border region. We have looked at it and seen the benefits in NI where they get a greater lion's share of the funding, and we often said it is a pity it is not down here. . . . IFI has made a huge impact in NI, but it has made a huge impact here in our town. We have all the new street scaping, and it is IFI funding being matched by the local authority. . . . Where we find the huge benefit for community development in IFI, it can make up 15 percent of what is needed by EU, in coming in as a partner, and with the group's own resources, the 25 percent can be easier got without putting a huge burden on the community that wouldn't have huge resources, rather than having to have a begging bowl or raising a loan in the bank. The IFI funding can be geared around to cushion it, as long as it is economically viable. We would love to see them not looking for the word "economically viable." The viability in community development can sometimes be very long-term. It can be ten years away. Investment in training [it] sometimes doesn't appear to show until maybe eight, nine, or ten years later.

Similar to the aforementioned Co. Monaghan group leader's praise of IFI development consultants, another community group leader from Co. Monaghan suggests that the consultants take a proactive approach by coming out to local communities to listen and to inspire them to put together proposals. He recognizes that the IFI consultant provided the incentives to get people moving along with the application package:

So in the meantime, we came across the IFI through a guy called Mr. X in Dundalk. He was newly appointed as a development consultant with them. He took the attitude of going out proactively to community groups. We have said it in print actually; we did something because of the ructions in Congress and so on about the IFI. If you remember there was a very serious debate. There was some congressman who started talking about the waste of money at the butterfly farm and that it failed. We said the IFI were the first people that came along and that they were prepared to listen and act proactively, and say "look, we think we can help you and we will find some way of helping because the town had been recognized at that stage statistically as the most hard-hit town in the whole border region." Those statistics show that forty-four businesses had closed and there was no earning. No area in Europe can quote that kind of statistic. So, within a couple of weeks through Mr. X, we got this person. He is based in the regional technical college in Dundalk and a girl lectures there and she put together a proposal for us and it went to the IFI and Interreg, and we got the funding to do jobs as it were . . . it is the same in any border region or any frontier region. We found this out when we read over the years about

Europe—like you have the very same problem as this in any other country about frontiers, you know the periphery. Central government seems to say, "Well look, leave them there." People in Fermanagh just across the border are saying the same thing about Belfast and London, different places, no-man's-land. Keep them out of that. So that is basically it.

Both the IFI and the EU Peace I funding package were set up to empower communities and give them hope. In contrast, the following interviews suggest that bureaucratic control over the funding process has to be streamlined. Moreover, additional IFI and EU Peace I funding agency development consultants need to be hired to work with grass-roots communities. Not surprisingly, local community groups evoke a convincing argument in favor of empowering local communities. This is most evident in the following narratives of the funding process by a number of community group leaders in the border region.

A community leader from Co. Fermanagh is of the opinion that there is too much bureaucracy and that too much of the aid is spent on administration. He believes that any future funding process has to streamline its bureaucracy so that it will be efficient in getting the funding down to the grass roots:

> What I see is there is far too much bureaucracy. Far too much of the money is wasted on pure administration. This is the old story, and it is up to the governments and international agencies to be absolutely ruthless on this. I mean, if you take the IFI and the EU Fund for Peace and Reconciliation, and you take the Border Area Authority, and that really is set up with no executive powers. It is supposed to be a co-coordinating body and I do not know if it has co-coordinated anything, but it is really set up as a sop to the EU to show that we have this bottom-up instead of top-down approach. But what is the point in setting something up for the sake of it if it has no executive teeth, if it cannot do anything?

Moreover, a community leader from Co. Monaghan believes that bureaucrats in Dublin do not understand what local community groups are attempting to accomplish. However, he argues that IFI and EU Peace I funding agency community development officers know very well the needs of local community groups:

> I would think a lot would go back just to the original thing of removing a lot of the layers of the bureaucracy. You send an application to Mr. X in Dublin sitting behind a desk. Now, Mr. X in Dublin does not even know what the project is about, and he possibly could not care less. His job is just to process the application as it comes in. Whereas the IFI and EU development officers, they talk to you. They know exactly what you want, the direction you want to go. And if you do not present it right,

as an ordinary community group of people, they are prepared to come back and question you about it. I think this is very important, and the more contact between the administrators of these funding agencies and the people who look at the applications . . . the more contact between them and the community groups, the better for all concerned.

Another community leader from Co. Monaghan also suggests that Irish government bureaucracy is determining which community groups get access to IFI and EU Peace I funding. He is of the opinion that any movement to empower local people is perceived by government officials as a revolution against central authority:

> Professor Arthur Robb did that right across the whole area. He kept at it, listening to people talking all the time. And one of the recommendations everyone said . . . this is a border fund, this Interreg fund, situated in the border . . . we need to create an authority independent of the civil service that would be administered and properly done. So Robb went back to them and put that kind of thing to them and criticized them heavily and was at the peace forum in Dublin as an example and he got the headlines for it . . . criticizing the two governments strongly, particularly the government in the South the way it was handling this money in this sense. So suddenly his contract ran out and he was not re-employed but they appointed a guy to be based in Monaghan, with Interreg, but Mr. X is an information officer.

He goes on to describe the contract between the funding agency and the community group in a negative manner because the funding process is too stringent and the money is too centralized. He believes that the pay-on-receipt of invoice payments makes life very difficult for poor community groups who don't have the cash to purchase necessary equipment:

> The way the normal funding system works, Peace and Reconciliation money is handed out to different delivery agencies, and there is one in the North, Cooperation North, and it is obviously business people and bankers and so on. There is the letter of offer, and that is something I am involved with. It is the worst legal document you can have. They fix it at 50 percent. They don't want to give for more than 50 percent, and what we are seeing is they pay on receipt of invoices-payments. They also at times want to see not only an auditor's report, but they want to see the actual bank statement of checks issued. So what happens is you spend £15,000, you wait, one, two, three, four, six months to get your £7,500, and this puts you into difficulty if you have to borrow. What happens with the IFI, or at least it did whilst we got our money off them, is that we got money up front. Once the thing was ratified, and it seemed to be properly done and everything else, the Credit Union, of course, came in and gave us our

money, with the result that we did those projects there with little or no bank interest, which makes it feasible. But you have to go into the bank for large sums of money. It is silly. Peace and Reconciliation do the same thing to some extent. They give some a percentage of your money up front and then the rest of it when you have satisfied them that the money has been properly spent. They have a report. . . . Now to the delivery of the money, as well in my own case of this Interreg money that is funding me at the moment. We got it at our first application in 1993–94. Now again it is a question of months waiting on the fund, so we reapplied again and we kept asking them. We originally applied for three years and they said a letter of contract went out for one year, and this is another thing people have been crying, crying out for. If you are seriously looking at this for one year or two years, you need continuity for at least five years if you are going to employ somebody. But they said, well I remember meeting the guy again one day and he said, "You might as well so you might as well apply." I applied again eventually. After I don't know how long, six, seven, or eight months, there came a letter of offer and I filled it in. After about two or three months, we got a check for the calendar year of 1996. We got the money for that in September dated back to January. As the conditions say, they pay the first quarter up front and on receipt then of invoices after that.

In addition, he suggests that people have local and creative ideas but are denied access to the funding by the technical nature of the funding application forms. He articulates the necessity of having more IFI and EU Peace I agency development consultants employed to work with local community groups to walk them through the application procedure:

We did criticize that a bit. In a sense that they nearly expected people to try too much and especially voluntary groups, which was giving up voluntary time to do too much, making it complicated for them. So what I think they are going to do is they are going to employ someone who would monitor it. It would be well worth it in my mind and help the people to fill in these assessments for Europe to prove, and I hope they do that because it will take a lot of worry off a load of people's minds. Again, I come back to the gamble of taking the chance. A lot of people would have an excellent idea and it would have worked except to see that they are intimidated by a lot of these technical forms. Again you go back to your great entrepreneur. They will do the business and they will make something work.

Similarly, a community leader from Co. Cavan perceived that funding agencies are working against the strategic interests of local community groups. He is of the opinion that people are voluntarily giving of their time, energy, and money, and their commitment is not recognized by central government. Also, he firmly believes that local people who are working for the needs of the community are bypassing county councils who feel threatened by community activists:

> But I do think myself that there is an awful lot of voluntary labor and everything else and money that correctly could be coming from bloody central government to help people to do things. It's just that it's all been channeled in and the day that stops, central government are in trouble then, to be honest . . . all the small business[es], all the areas like that . . . Well, the way the thing is done at the present time . . . See what happens here was they lost the rates so everything went back to central government and before this they allocated so much money to roads, so much money for sewage, etc. There is no money to allocate now because when they get their money now it's decided before they get it from whatever funding they get it from and where it is going to be spent . . . I can see the local county councillors don't know where they stand at the present time because they seem to have lost their bit of ground, and groups like us have taken over from them, and we are doing our own thing. We are no longer going to those people and trying to push them to do something for us. We are able to do it for ourselves at the present time.

He goes on to say:

> Well, I think it should go direct to the communities involved with the necessary controls in place, the same as the controls of the county council. I mean I think that we would spend our money a hell of a sight better here if we got it direct from the county council spending whatever money they are spending in the area. I honestly believe that, but again why should they consider that the guy is more capable of handling the actual cash coming in than I am? Okay, I may go with fifty thousand but the guy in the county council goes fifty thousand just if you put the proper controls in place. There is no reason why cash can't come directly to a community group like us. It's coming now from IFI directly to us. If it's going to the local authorities like you know and the money is going to be spent the same, I think this local authority should be structured in such a way that a representative from each community group is on the local council like. How about you elect them and hopefully they are elected as the local community representative on the council or that there's some way that at every meeting there, that there is one or two people can go in and put their case forward and make submissions at local meetings.

A community group leader from Co. Fermanagh believes that there are too many committees and too much of the money is spent on administration. Any future funding process needs to have its bureaucracy streamlined to be most efficient in getting the money to where it is supposed to go, and go quickly:

One of the things I feel (and this is where I put on my hardheaded business hat . . . I think a lot) . . . whether it is the International Fund, or the fund for Peace and Reconciliation, or any other sort of grant aid, I feel maybe there is too much emphasis on projects which are far too socially oriented. I would like to see a situation where the total package is distributed on more viable projects, projects with more possibility of being self-sustaining in the long term. In other words, instead of slicing the cake into a hundred parts, I would slice it maybe into twenty, and they would be good projects with people who have some track record, some possibility of succeeding. I am a firm believer that if you give the people a taste for success in pure material terms, I'm sorry to have to say, that will help big time. I mean that is not a panacea to cure the problem, but it is a big part of it, and the other thing that is important is and I see this, is bureaucracy . . . I would be on the board of the Shannon-Erne Waterway, the County Enterprise Fund Company, a few things like that. What I see is there is far too much bureaucracy, far too much of the money wasted on pure administration. This is the old story and it is up to the governments and international agencies to be absolutely ruthless on this.

The following statements exemplify the responses of some of the community leaders in the border region illustrating the political disempowerment of local communities by Belfast and Dublin. This community leader from Co. Fermanagh is cynical with regard to the British government's distribution of funds. He suggests that both governments are using IFI and EU Peace I money to support government projects to the detriment of local communities:

It would be a common perception that the criteria bind us. I think that is a common perception among all the people ourselves, everybody who is rejected for money. I am privileged to see it from both sides of the fence, sitting on the local partnership board, and obviously in a competitive situation. When you are maybe six, seven, maybe nine times oversubscribed, a lot of people are going to be rejected. One of the big problems with European funding is that people get the document and they immediately see that there are a number of criteria—disadvantaged area, border region, cross-community, private sector and public sector, that is us, tick every box. We must qualify, fill in an application, and lots of people did put in applications for businesses even and they put them into the Department of Finance and Personnel, and like that they just got a letter back. The first thing that has to be said about Peace and Reconciliation money, again it won't be challenged because there is not the political mechanisms to challenge. What did the arms of government do with the money they got from the Peace and Reconciliation fund? It was obscene what the Department of Agriculture, the Tourist Board, and the Department of Economic Development got the money for. I am convinced that the arms of government North and South but particularly North are up to their oxters in European funding and their arm in the kitty, followed closely, I might add by the universities trying to muscle in and get their armful because they are the supreme experts at Eurospeak. I have been trying to ingratiate myself with the University of Ulster because I feel that they probably could restructure my application in words that would yield. It is all about the use of words, and use of buzzwords, and that nowadays. I have sympathy for the people in communities who feel they have an excellent application. What happens in a lot of communities I think, particularly in the Protestant communities more so, that they are not well versed in the whole process of applying for money because they have certain barriers to get over. There were various objections, which you are obviously well aware of, and they were reluctant, but they are ready to come in now, and they are putting in applications. The applicants to the funders I hear are mediocre and poor because they are not seasoned applicants like some bigger organizations who are in there and know exactly where to get it. And some of the Intermediary Funding Bodies have been the worst. They have been the biggest culprits. Equally, there is another danger that I feel and I don't know how to get round this and I know on our partnership we can't favor one over the other, but certainly we are trying to use all our might to accommodate and make allowances for applicants coming from the Protestant community.

He adds that statutory agencies and the bureaucracy have too much power in the distribution of funds, and this is very frustrating for local community groups who feel that the criteria of the funds limit the scope and breadth of their creative ideas:

Now some of the people would have felt that, well we would want this organization to call the agencies into question to challenge them in the best possible way. But the reality has been, and that is frustrating some of our members that, because we are being funded by them, we end up that we can't challenge anything and we just carry on doing what they dictate has to be done, which is far removed from we as business people know what should be done. But because what we want to do is practical, hands on, down to earth, meeting the real needs, the realities of the area, they don't see that as measurable or quantifiable, or evaluative or whatever they want and they want to run programs. As long as you project your program . . . the problem is that every program under the sun has been thought of by now, and when you go with it, you find that it has already been done, and they don't want that. No one knows better than I do, at this stage in organization. We are just at our wit's end with bureaucracy and slowness. . . . Bureaucracy, pure bureaucracy and you see there is a lot of lip service for community activism and patronizing lip service, and I use the word patronizing very, very carefully and guardedly. "What good people you are, you business people coming here taking up your time to run Fermanagh Business Initiative, and you do much more. We didn't realize you were doing so much." And then they leave you to rot in hell in the hope that you will go away. They don't want the fast pace of a business agenda. We are just stifled in this country with bureaucracy, and the other thing of course, it is fueled by the fact that we are here in a political vacuum. The truest words that Baroness Denton ever spoke, as the economy minister for NI, was after she had resigned or after she was defeated, when she became embroiled in controversy about the NI Civil Service. She said that "the problem with NI was that the civil servants ruled it." She never spoke a truer word. There is no accountability, the ministers that we have are not elected here, and the MPs are really immaterial. They have no power. It is only ministers who have power at the end of the day, and we are far removed. It is really the scourge of the whole economy of NI. The whole thing being run by the civil service and they do run the show, they do run the show.

In addition, another community group leader from Derry outlines why he thinks that it is important to build the capacity of local groups so that they can master the language of the bureaucracy to access funds. His portrayal of the government's use of IFI and EU Peace I funding in lieu of government spending in NI suggests a vivid and subtle awareness of the intricate political maneuvering of former prime minister John Major's Tory government:

One of the big problems that fit the community sector, the social economy sector, when people try to access money from any funding source, is that the level of bureaucracy can be quite difficult, and the language, which they use, can be quite difficult. . . . Now there is a view that giving the nature of the funding cycle that lots of the money was being targeted and brought into the North of Ireland as an "objective one region." The money actually hasn't come in and what lots of people [believe], and there is evidence of this, [is] that the British government have in many ways utilized IFI and European monies as a substitute to what they actually should be doing themselves. So I think that we have to insist that monies from the IFI should be continued. I think that the money from Europe should be continued, but they should be actually viewed as additional money to help us come up with innovative ways of actually building up our local community's economy. I think that there has been evidence that [that is] where monies have been used by the British government in the past. I think that there is a big dispute going on at the moment in terms of Peace and Reconciliation money, which has come from Europe, through the Department of Agriculture for Northern Ireland (DANI), which was using monies for DANI projects as opposed to rural development projects.

In contrast, a community leader from Co. Monaghan wonders who will actually benefit from local community development. He articulates whether tourists from Europe and North America rather than local people will really benefit from the economic regeneration of border communities. He questions whether Ireland will become Europe's "Magic Kingdom." However, he thinks that the Shannon-Erne Waterway development is a noteworthy project that was worth funding:

> We know the chap that is the officer with Interreg, Mr. X. We know that he is a fantastic fella, and he has done work around Belfast and out on the Aran Islands and everything. But the Department of Finance must have put their foot on his neck because he is not doing the job we thought he would be able to do. But then it is crazy. He is covering all of NI and the border counties. One officer covering all that territory, working out of an office in Monaghan, it is ludicrous you know. It is crazy . . . oftentimes we look to him, and we say, "Whom really are we doing these things for? Are we doing it for the European Community rather than for ourselves? Who is going to benefit from this? Is it going to be Germans and people from Holland?" They can come and have a better time. Give you ten years' tax incentive and there is a green field site. The benefits would be a lot quicker, but then long term they could be gone. But the Shannon-Erne Waterway will be there in a hundred years' time, and still be doing the job it is supposed to do. I could not figure that one out; whether it is grand for the rich German or the person from Holland or whether it is for the boy standing on the riverbank with his Wellingtons on him, and he has not got much more money in his pocket.

Another community group leader from Co. Monaghan believes that statutory agencies are not in tune with the needs of local community groups who feel isolated from local authorities. Local rural border communities feel isolated, ignored, and cut off from central government. According to this person, this feeling of disconnectedness and alienation has resulted in a loss of morale in local communities:

> But by far the biggest question I think for rural communities, for development groups, is in that whole area of capacity building. That means a lot more quality training, a lot more development officers working with these groups and very definitely reaching out to groups. A lot of the statutory agencies have no idea of this at all. They say we are here for you. Now we are here for you. But the people who need help by tradition are the people who won't come for it . . . so it is very difficult. We have no government minister and that's a very significant factor. If there is a government minister in any constituency in Southern Ireland, then the government funds go there. Roads get done, health service gets done, education services get done, etc. If you haven't got a government minister, you are way down the line in priority. That reality, you might wish it otherwise, it might seem a cynical comment but that is fact. If you were to look at it you see the loops there that we have got. How do we get over that difficulty? And that is very real without a government minister or anything like that. How do we

get ourselves heard? It's very difficult. We have to work about ten times harder than anybody else to get ourselves heard.

Another community group leader from Co. Monaghan also suggests that bureaucrats in Dublin do not really know or understand what local community groups are trying to do. However, funding agency development officers are in touch with and know the needs of local community groups:

> I would think a lot would go back just to the original thing of removing a lot of the layers of the bureaucracy. As far as I would see it now, I would think that both Mr. X [IFI] comes from the initial stages and Mr. W [EU Peace I] at this stage, would come and talk to a group. I think they'd talk to a group, and when they leave, the group is able to talk to them again, if you know what I mean. The application goes in after that. Now if the application is not for the group we are talking about, they may come back and say, "Look, will you clarify this or that for us?" . . . They get the picture. They know exactly. Now Mr. W has been involved over a number of years and if I called Mr. W tomorrow and said, "We want something for such a thing," he would know what you were talking about before the application comes in at all. You would have to make the application, I am not saying you would not have to, but Mr. W would know exactly what I was talking about on the phone before you get the application together because he is in touch with the group from day one and he knows what is going on.

These respondents perceive that the British and Irish governments are using IFI and EU Peace I funds for government projects rather than local community projects. They interpreted this political maneuvering as a need to maintain administrative control over local politics.

In summary, these community group leaders are enthusiastic supporters of empowering local communities to be entrepreneurial, recognizing that the bureaucracy needs to be streamlined from the funding process. It is not difficult to believe that community group leaders in Derry also hold similar ideas about the empowerment of local communities.

Implicit in a Derry community leader's story is the view that Loyalist and Republican ex-political prisoners are marginalized and discriminated against by the British government. For example, he argues ex-prisoner efforts to find employment are thwarted by government because they have been convicted of a criminal offense:

> One of the pitfalls is, for example, to teach in the North, you need a Diploma of Education. There is no bar to anybody getting that Diploma of Education, but to get on the course, you must be funded by the Department of Education in the North [DENI]. . . . It is those type of things that

we have tried to articulate. Much in the same way, and I have said this, we live in areas of high unemployment. We do not want to create the situation that ex-prisoners, that just because you come out of jail, that somehow that you go to the top of an unemployment list, when there is some fella waiting ten years for a job and has not got it. There is an inequality, which has to be addressed that we have to compete within.

He believes that grant application forms for the district partnership and the Department of the Environment (DOE) are complex, and the agencies have rotating officers, which makes it very difficult for groups to make and maintain working relationships. The Northern Ireland Voluntary Trust (NIVT), on the other hand, is very efficient and fast to process applications:

My experience is that the ex-prisoners group did not find it very straightforward. Certainly, when it comes to some of your costing, you needed a wee bit of help. But in the main NIVT forms, it was very straightforward. The way it was handled was very efficient and the distribution of money was very speedy. The district partnership in Derry, which is run more than the council, and the DOE is the opposite. They are very bureaucratic. The forms are very, very complicated. They see the employed persons on short-term contracts, its facilitators and, whereas, they themselves are very confident and very sound people, you are dealing with a new one. We have dealt with two or three in the period of a year and each one of them they come in. I will give you an example. We set down a constitution, our aims and objectives, our bank statement, etc. About four months later we were asked for the same thing. We were saying, "We already done this." They were coming back and saying, "So you did." They will phone you now, and say "Can we have your most recent bank statement? The last one you have is two months old." We would say, "The bank we work with sends out a bank statement every three months." We are not a big organization. We don't need a weekly bank statement, because the numbers of bank transactions we have are minimal. We would need the ones from last week, but we work with the bank and they send out a statement every three months, and it is more than adequate. They seem to be very bureaucratic. Sometimes, they are very intimidated by what they are doing, right, in the sense of the politics of it. The district partnership would be made up of people who would reflect the community. There is Unionist councillors; there is Republican councillors, etc. We know from experience that there is this sort of thing. You can nearly hear someone saying that there is danger. So you have facilitators coming in and they are trying to make sure at the end of the day that everything is right, every I is dotted and every T is stroked. A good example of it is that the Derry Taxi Association put in a bid for money for a disabled taxi, and they got a letter of offer about last November, and this is July and they got no money to buy it. That type of slowness. Whereas, the NIVT, because I remember when Ms. X came down to visit us, the first grant we got was three thousand pounds. There was a group of eight or nine of us managing it at the time and we got that three thousand pounds. It took us about two or three months to make up our mind on what we were going to buy with it because it is the first time we got that amount of money. Now obviously we are relaxing into it and I think it is the opposite from the partnership. They are actually too slow, and some of the things that they do is that if you apply for funding to do something, say like you apply for funding for a photocopier, they would turn around and say to you, "Buy your photocopier and then we will give you the money." People have argued and argued successfully, saying if you had the money to buy the photocopier, then we wouldn't be asking you for the funding. What you should be doing is saying "yes." We need a photocopier. There is the check, and away you go and buy it. They will do the opposite, they will do this sort of thing of "You get the photocopier, get us the invoices and get us the receipts and everything and we will get you the money." Needy groups, they are not in a position to do that. They actually done that in relation to the taxi, asking the Taxi Association to buy the taxi, and they would send out the money, instead of saying, "Right, give an estimate from two garages, how much the car is going to cost and then we will see to it."

Similarly, another community leader from Derry ponders whether the Department of Finance and Personnel (DFP) in Belfast really understands the basic human needs of local communities, making it difficult for community groups to get access to economic assistance. This is what he had to say on the issue:

I think that it is particularly difficult at the moment to get money out of Europe. And the reason why it is very, very difficult, I would lay blame squarely at the door of the apparatus that is currently particularly within the North of Ireland, that is, under the control of the British Exchequer. We have a department that monitors everything here and the DFP has got a particular mind-set that is not au fait with the needs of local communities. They believe in a particular ethos, which is about the conventional approach to economics. They have a mind-set which talks about measurement in terms of jobs created, bums in seats in terms of training, where people at a local level are actually saying "Look, there are no jobs." . . . When applications come in from these organizations, they don't understand them. So what they do is put up hurdles in their way, and it is very, very difficult. . . . So, what we are saying is that it is extremely difficult to get money out of the system. Which means then what happens to its groups on the ground? They get extremely frustrated. They are saying these programs have been set up to do X, Y, and Z. And that local groups then tend to do, because they don't see the faceless men and women of DFP.

He also notes that local people's awareness of their grassroots economy has to be considered by the funding agencies when they put together the funding process:

A lot of groups are now moving from community development into community economic development and this is causing some concern, because it means that people are now challenging the status quo. What they are challenging for the first time is that those who have been charged with economic development have got it wrong and don't like to be threatened.

Another community leader from Derry argues that local communities are organized and willing to accept economic funding from both funding agencies:

I suppose there are many groups. The one good thing about Ireland in general is that there is really a vibrant community politics. Community action, I think, is quite developed in comparison to other countries. Maybe this is a reflection of the sort of political depth of it, so much as they are open to the conflict, especially in the North.

He goes on to indicate his concern about the government's conduct in the distribution of EU Peace I funds within NI. He discusses public expenditure cuts and the quality of employment emerging out of the peace package:

We were shouting about this last Christmas when the public expenditure cuts were made. Cuts in health, cuts in education, cuts in employment training, all areas that would have been funded through the peace package in some shape or form that was the kind of arguments we were making. So that is undermining the idea of additional issues. While there would be new projects going on, there are also old projects collapsing. So I think that has to be recognized. And we have said [this] directly to the European commissioner Monica Wolf-Mattheus. We have written to her and explained to her our analysis of the situation; that it was always said it had to be additional. I think the present government, how they are going to manage the economy, is unclear, and I think on top of that there is some doubts about the quality of the appointments that is coming out to this city. While there are jobs, I think there is now a bottoming-out of the unemployment rate. There is an additional amount of work and again for the sake of arguing, I think there is something about the quality of the jobs currently: part-time, low-pay type of jobs, mostly women who are sometimes second, third, or more often only who are sometimes receiving assistance. So, I think that the quality of employment has got to be looked at.

Similarly, another community leader from Derry advocates that economic funding must empower both working-class communities who are engaged in the cockpit of the conflict:

There are actually real issues involved here. There are also issues of power and money, and employment and power within the society. I just think that external funding should actually be concentrating on inequality within the society. That does not mean that all the money should go to the Nationalist community, but it would by definition mean that money would be going to empower working-class communities and to let those communities set their own agendas.

Another community group leader from Derry thinks that the Troubles are a symptom of the pain and despair held by working-class Protestants and Catholics who feel despondent with little hope and no real future to look forward to:

I think it's happening again, whereby groups that are not particularly skilled, who had resources for years, they obviously have community support. Here they are now, maybe they're made brief, maybe they're made a better administrative battle and had professionals to go in and help them, rather than the bureaucrats, with layers and layers and layers of paperwork, which is actually very extreme and intimidating to people's self-esteem and self-confidence. We are not all part-time solicitors and accountants and lawyers—those types, and know our way through the funding minefield. There is a language. There are buzzwords giving applications that seem to set signals off and are more acceptable than people running around with needs and delusions. It's not a prediction, but I would argue that pre-1969, the Bogside, Shantallagh, the Creggan, the Brandywell, Nationalist districts, parts of Irish Street, Tullyalley, New Buildings, which is a Nationalist district, Ballymacrory, they have f—k all. It's 1997, and they still have f—k all. So in the gap in between, somebody failed to transfer, to transform those Christians. Somebody had their mind-set that those people were the lowest of the low, weren't worth bothering with, and they did nothing for them. They grew up on housing estates with no facilities, no amenities, nothing, and then they're wondering why the teenagers vandalize and wreck things when they get to fifteen and sixteen years of age. If those are the hounds men who are spurring Derry onward or, spurring any district onward, then they are a bit wind-filled. Who are your friends, who's acceptable, who's respectable, what's a good, quiet, passive community group?

Implicit in an IFI border area consultant's story is the view that, in the past, Protestants have been distrustful of the IFI. The IFI emerged out of the 1985 AIA, and was seen as a political tool of Nationalist America to maneuver loyal Ulstermen into a United Ireland. This is what he had to say about the issue:

Yes, I would agree to a great extent with that thesis and not just my experience working with the fund but having worked within NI with both communities—Catholic and Protestant. There is a cultural difference and there is also then, of course, specifically in relation to the fund, the association with the AIA that has caused a problem at the outset, and it did mean that while equal effort has been made to encourage projects to develop in both communities that a number of Unionist district councils, for example, would not deal with IFI for a number of years. That now is no longer the case, so there is a catching-up process going on and it would be the case [with] the Nationalist communities. I think the cultural differences here would be probably much more inclined toward looking to economic development on a communal basis than the Protestant communities. There would be a more independent stand-alone characteristic in the Protestant community than in the Catholic community maybe, although that would not be borne out by the pattern of distribution. For example, Derry cooperatives in the past showed that the small creamery co-op would have been equally distributed between Catholic and Protestant areas, and I am talking about back in the 1920s or earlier in the century. But Derry Cooperative would have always been pragmatic and the business would have gone sour because they have got the cooperation to handle it, so it might not be a good illustration of the cultural characteristics of the two communities. But yes, I would say even with my dealing here in the southern border counties where you have a much more homogeneous Catholic community by and large, but nevertheless, there is evidence of the pockets of high-level Protestant people in the South. They would be slow to come forward with projects for economic development but that is changing now, and I can think of a number of cases where we would have quite strong Protestant entries in some border counties where now we are going to follow this course as well.

A community group leader from Co. Fermanagh also emphasizes the importance of IFI monies in building up the infrastructure of small towns and villages. Now the Protestant community wants some of the IFI money from the United States:

Within community groups, the general observation would be that IFI money has gone into big business, because that is where you see the signs up all over the place, and yes it has gone into their urban development program. There were a few hiccups at the start but in all fairness I think it has done. I know speaking here in the town of Enniskillen, it has benefited tremendously, tremendously from IFI investment. It sometimes takes outsiders to tell us about what a wonderful town it is, and that would not have been the case before IFI investment. "Okay," cynics will say, "people with money get money." The IFI didn't pay for all of the work. You had to be able to put up a substantial amount of money yourself to be able to draw on the IFI grant. This is what the IFI is best known for, that and the CRISP [Community Regeneration Improvement Special Program] schemes. It has been mainly targeted at smaller towns and villages and they generally are careful that there is only one application per village, and in conjunction with the Department of the Environment they have done a lot of regenerative work of villages, and very good regeneration work. You take the likes of Belleek, Irvinestown, initially the Protestant villages were not benefiting because there was no mechanism, there was nobody coming forward with applications. But that is changing and they are coming forward now, and as somebody piped up from the back of a hall at a meeting, "How do we get our hands on some of this Fenian money," because that is the way it is perceived. It was perceived as Fenian money coming from America. I think the IFI is making very strenuous efforts to correct that image.

In contrast, another group leader from Derry is of the opinion that the EU Peace I Fund is trying very hard to be inclusive and introduce participatory democracy at the grassroots level. For example, he thinks that the partnership boards are forcing people from both sides of the sectarian divide to work together to allocate resources to the community:

Then how the IFBs and NI Voluntary Trust, those bodies have set up advisory groups to advise them about allocating the funds and keeping it open and transparent, honest, clear and also helping people with their application follow-up work, support work etc.–Europe and the partnership boards. I mean, there's problems with all partnership boards I know . . . but the principle still stands that it was a great effort, physical effort . . . I don't know, an alternative interest on the word that would employ something devious in this half of Europe.

He suggests that brokerage politics ensures that those community groups "in the know" are taken care of, and this cuts across all of the funding agencies. Seasoned groups know whom to contact, whereas new groups may not have the confidence to call up the agencies to find out the status of their application:

To be honest there is a bit of that in it. I mean, when you have met me now, you will associate me with this building and if you find out I am a nice guy, come in with a cup of coffee, lovely chocolate biscuits, lovely day, you will have a nice memory of us. So then the next time I ring you up and say, "Have you any slippage money?" that it is the end of the year you could have budgeted, rung you up "Have you money?" I have the confidence to do that. I know how your system works. I know that you have to spend your budget. I know that come March you are looking for money. I need a computer or I need a new office refurbished or I need something. I ring you up, "How's it going, mate, are you happy, it's a grand day, how's your wife and the kids, have you any money?" So associate me with the project and you give us the money. All the programs are very much the same. Those well-experienced community workers know the systems, know how they work, how you get in there. You got to get the proposal. You could write a nice letter, they can lobby you, one thing or another. Of course you'll get the money, whereas those organizations who are trying to start up, they have got to go for the application forms for a variety of projects. It is so convoluted. They don't have the confidence to run up and hassle or to put a wee bit of pressure on, or to say a few right words in the right place. These guys aren't going to get as much money. So, there is that element and attitude.

Moreover, another community group leader from Derry has a pretty clear understanding of the power of NI's civil service in the distribution of EU Peace I funds. He believes that community economic development means professional development. This is what he had to say:

Very little of the European money comes direct to organizations. It is nearly all filtered through the civil service here. Although, there have been efforts by the EU of late to try and make sure that the NI civil service does not manage the money. It is very difficult to bypass the civil service in that whole network. We are very conscious of their position of power. We do quite well, but we really have to use the system, and John Hume's office would keep us informed. We have people in NI who work in Europe and we lift the phone. It is not difficult. We don't range through all of the grants that are available from Europe. We just see what grants are applicable to the effective work we do, which is professional community development, and at the minute, development is actually hooked onto our basic philosophy, which is people only go when given the opportunity of accepting responsibility.

Another community group leader from Derry emphasizes that the DFP doesn't understand the needs of local communities—unemployment, poverty, and deprivation—as groups find it hard to get money out of the system. This is what he had to say on the issue:

When applications come in from these organizations, they don't understand them, so what they do is put up hurdles in their way, and it is very, very difficult. A good example would be, there is a major European initiative here in the city at the moment called the Urban Initiative, which was specifically set up to focus resources in the Creggan, which is a dominantly Nationalist-Republican area of high unemployment and deprivation. The Bogside and Brandywell area, again an area of high unemployment and deprivation, also seen as a Nationalist-Republican area, also the Fountain, which is a small Protestant working-class area, which also has high levels of poverty and deprivation. Now these three communities, what they have got in common are unemployment, poverty, and deprivation. They have been trying to access money from this program, which was launched just over two years ago, and the money hasn't hit the streets yet. It is because DFP insists on what they call economic appraisals of their projects, that they are putting it through a number of economists. They are putting it through an economist with DOE, who may well approve it, but before he releases the money he has them put it up to the DFP. After developing all of the relationships through the IFI and organizations like Northern Ireland Co-operative Development Agency (NICDA), and trying to break down the barriers, and understanding the bureaucracy which the DOE has to operate under, they have built up the relationship then, their economist has approved the project. But now, all of a sudden, they are accountable to the DFP, and they have to send it to the second economist, who has not been through the learning curve, and the whole process stops. So, what we are saying is that it is extremely difficult to get money out of the system, which means then what happens to its groups on the ground gets extremely frustrated. They are saying these programs have been set up to do X, Y, and Z and that the local groups then tend to do, because they don't see the faceless men and women of DFP. They see the civil servant who is actually in the DOE. They see organizations like NICDA, who are actually out trying to help, and they see the community activists like the Bogside and Belmore Initiative or the Creggan Partnership or the Gasshare Trust, and they become the point of conflict within the local community. "You are all bluster, but nothing is happening." So we are then blamed for the slowness of the process, and the real problem rests with DFP. . . . A lot of groups are now moving from community development into community economic development, and this is causing some concern, because it means that people are now challenging the status quo, and what they are challenging for the first time is that those who have been charged with economic development have got it wrong and don't like to be threatened.

Moreover, he maintains that statutory agencies must carefully devise an effective policy for local community development:

I also think we need to have capacity building of people in statutory bodies to understand grassroots organizations. I think if there was a program around that I think it would obviously bear fruit. I also believe that there should be an effective policy that coordinates local economic development. Now I am biased. I actually believe that if anybody is looking at global economics and they look at particular problems that we see within the United States in terms of communities moving from one region to another following the wind, and in their wake they are leaving communities that are devastated, so therefore, how do you actually build up those communities?

Another community group leader from Derry is of the opinion that economic aid from the funding agencies has assisted local communities to create employment opportunities for their residents and include citizens to participate in the decision-making process of how the money should be spent. He fears that if the Peace I approach is not successful, then the voluntary community sector will be scapegoated and blamed for its failure:

I suppose it is a very difficult question to answer, because when you actually see the results of it, you see it today or do you see it in five or ten years time, and is it acceptable to say we see it in five years' time, therefore, we don't look at the way it is at the minute. I have seen a lot of community groups working in really disadvantaged areas who have got themselves some resources and have been about to do what would never have been allowed to happen. And it is supporting people who they would never have otherwise supported at a local level and I think that is good. I think it is important and I think people will benefit and are currently benefiting from those projects. I have seen projects set up by local people creating jobs, and creating employment opportunities within that community for themselves and that they don't get the support from the training and agencies or the government employment body because they are saying "we are not accrediting you as an employment training project because you don't fit within our guidelines," and yet this is a training site. They are up against a difficult situation. They are doing stuff which I think is currently benefiting individuals within their community and I think in turn will benefit more individuals within that community, and there will be a sense of ownership of the community organization of who does what. In a sense, it invests in community participation, because that invests in political democracy and we have not really looked at how you get out of people being more interested in their community and for their community organizations. How do they become more interested and participate more in democracy? And we have not looked at if there is a way to show how you get out of people being more understood in their community and for their community organizations. How do they become more into democracy? Is there a way to do it? Currently, we have got the district partnerships, but that is a group of people elected through the years; and, several people involved from the voluntary sector, so it gives you some idea. . . . They are beginning to say, "Well, there is a kind of a model for participation, which we want to increase in the future." I think more and more people are saying, "Yeah, we must get our community involved. We must ensure that there is more involvement." And I think it will be a few years before they can really judge how that manifests and whether community development has been successful. I mean I have a current concern, which is that because there are a lot of question marks over whether the Peace and Reconciliation fund is actually benefiting the people, or is the peace and reconciliation due to the peace package? It will be the community voluntary sector that will remain if the answer to that question is no. It will be the scapegoat. The community in Belfast will be scapegoated if it is viewed that the peace and reconciliation did not come up due to social inclusion. I think if that happened, that would be a real undermining implication of the peace package, and it does take a number of years to actually include that. You have all the community development going on, but in 1999, all these community organizations will be gone, and that knowledge is not helpful at this time, rather than saying that the community organizations like to get money to sustain them.

In summary, some of the respondents illustrate the necessity of shifting power away from government bureaucracy to the grassroots level. Moreover, they highlight the centrality of power and centralized decision making as critical issues in the distribution and control of funds. It would appear that the experience of our respondents has been a major determinant in their attitudes toward the whole funding process. On the other hand, some of the respondents suggest that the funding agencies are deliberately allocating resources to the middle class and noncontroversial community leaders within both communities as well as exercising bureaucratic control over the processing of applications. Finally, others suggest that both funds have assisted in restoring pride to local communities, while others contend that "single-identity" economic needs must be worked on within both communities before they can work together across the sectarian divide.

DISCUSSION

This chapter has illustrated some of the issues that community groups, civil servants, and development officers find to be salient about both funding agencies. Undoubtedly, the economic roots of conflict must be addressed if a sustainable peace is to be built and a new social contract forged among ethnopolitical groups in a postconflict society (Junne and Verkoren 2004).

First, the respondents highlighted tension between local ownership of community projects and local and national government. The voluntary sector has empowered local citizens to engage in participatory democratic activities. The Troubles were a symptom of despair of the poor and the marginalized especially in border areas. In providing hope to local communities, the proactive work of the voluntary sector has challenged the political status quo. Respondents suggest that local district and county councils are locked in a power struggle with local community groups as local government officials fear losing their power. Local community group leaders were concerned that the voluntary sector would be scapegoated if the economic assistance failed to bring about peace.

Consequently, the politicization and activity of local community groups may have affected the behavior of government agencies at the national and local level who perceive these groups to be challenging the status quo, thereby changing the hierarchical relationship between government and the people. The activation of the grass roots, therefore, has created stresses and strains between itself and the central bureaucracy. Consequently, another factor that may be crucial for the success of local community empowerment and transformation is that economic regeneration is not a top-down governmental process. If local economies are to be reactivated and the nature of the conflict transformed, funding agencies must also recognize the importance of working closely with local communities. This relationship stands outside the hegemonic control of local and central government. The border community group leaders suggest that the availability of IFI and EU Peace I Fund development officers and consultants and direct access by community groups to both funds are critical and important successes of the funding process. The fact that these respondents see the importance of accessibility to community development officers and consultants illustrates the salience of personal contact within Ireland's political culture. Finally, the repackaging of community needs and issues into application proposals that both appease the agency and gain access for a particular group to the economic assistance is an issue that has surfaced time and again during the course of these interviews.

Second, respondents indicated that agency development officers were building trust and local partnerships between community groups and the funding agencies. Development officers serve the needs of local communities by actively listening, nurturing, and inspiring project leaders while respecting their dignity as they aim for the stars. Development officers provide an important safety valve between the grass roots and the funding agencies and local and central government. In general, respondents also indicated the necessity of placing more development officers on the ground to work with local community groups.

Third, in their narratives respondents emphasized the conflictual relationship that exists between the bureaucracy and local community groups who feel isolated and marginalized from local and central governments. They insisted that the centrality of power and decision making limits the entrepreneurial spirit and creative spark of local communities. Frustration manifests itself in the perceptions that the civil service, which is not in tune with local needs, erects barriers through a complex application process that drains the energy of local groups.

Thus, an extremely important element that this research brings to light is the feeling among community development groups that centralized bureaucracies do have too much control over the funding process. For example, community groups in border areas suggest that statutory agencies are not in tune with local communities and that the bureaucracy has too much power over the funding process. Also, community groups in Derry suggest that not all EU Peace I Fund monies that go through the NI civil service are going into marginalized and deprived areas. The funding agencies are playing it safe by supporting groups deemed to have credibility within their respective communities. These respondents appear to believe that the central bureaucracy in both Belfast and Dublin have too much control over the funding process. Further, they suggest that the administration of the funding process must be streamlined.

On the other hand, civil servants feel that both IFI and EU Peace I funding is indeed reaching down into the communities and bypassing entanglement by central government. The concern of funding agency development officers revolves around the problem of what happens to these groups once the funding process terminates.

Community groups on both sides of the border and in Derry believe that the EU Peace I Fund application process is too complex, too rigid, and has too many criteria. Some of these group leaders also suggest that IFI funds go directly into the local communities. However, an overall critique of both funding agencies by these respondents suggests that those groups with personal contacts with persons within the funding agencies receive the money. Localism and personalism within the local political culture ensures that those "in the know" get access to economic resources.

Fourth, the respondents illuminated the necessity of building both the human and intercommunal security and economic capacity of each community by replacing the war economy with a sustainable economic infrastructure. Respondents intimated that central government funds projects from middle-class applicants while ignoring the plight of the poor. In addition, they implied that the single-identity economic needs of each community must be met before Protestants and Catholics move toward collaborating on joint economic development projects.

Fifth, respondents centered their attention on the politicization of who benefits from the economic assistance. There was a general feeling that the people who volunteer their time are contributing to the renaissance of a vibrant community politics and activism. However, they cautioned that while seasoned community groups are successfully accessing the funds,

Protestants who are not yet fully versed in the funding process perceive that Catholics are receiving all of the economic assistance. This perception is in part an indication of the current decline in Protestant support for the 1998 GFA. Protestants perceive that Catholics are accruing all of the economic benefits, which they see as unjust and unreasonable, which further confirms their suspicions of a Catholic plot that becomes an integral part of the collective siege mentality of the Protestant community. As a result, respondents were of the opinion that it is difficult to encourage Protestants to participate in cross-community projects. They also mentioned that individuals doing cross-community work are targeted by the various paramilitary organizations. Moreover, they felt that ex-prisoners and border communities were alienated and marginalized by the lack of quality of the employment opportunities created. Some respondents were of the opinion that economic aid undermined the Republican armed struggle, and in order to form new identities and develop a new social contract, political issues must be addressed before real sustainable reconciliation can take place in NI.

Sixth, funding agencies are stimulating employment opportunities to forge the development of responsible democracy within a new representative civil society. Some pundits will point to the decline in the rate of political violence as the aid has nurtured cross-community contacts enhancing the quality of life and level of optimism in both communities promoting a fertile political ground to support the implementation of the GFA. Economic aid has restored pride and recharged the self-esteem and belief in local communities. Respondents indicated that as a result of events taking place on the ground, both communities are getting a "fair crack of the whip." In particular, it was perceived that Catholics who suffered the economic brunt of the Troubles had an ethos and culture of community action that allowed them to be proactive in applying and securing funds from the funding agencies.

In contrast, the images of other respondents indicated that the assistance was not targeting disadvantaged areas since the cycle of intergenerational unemployment continued unabated. In addition, they verified that special interest groups such as the universities and large farmers had the connections and know-how to access the funding agencies so that the process of peacemaking had become a business. Community development is a slow, tedious process that can impact the overall feeling of hope in a community. They expressed a concern that ongoing community projects will not sustain themselves once the funds dry up.

Seventh, one of the most striking findings that this research brings to light is how political culture influences perceptions found especially among community group leaders on the Republic of Ireland side of the border. Culture is a locally shared common sense based on past knowledge and traditional values and ideas that impact the way people think and feel about their reality (Avruch 1998; Cohen 1999). In high cultural context societies like the Republic of Ireland, nonverbal communication, group harmony, and identity are an integral part of everyday life (Lederach 1995). Localism and personalism are unique aspects of this high-context interdependent society (Chubb 1992). Consequently, most respondents from the Republic of Ireland suggest that IFI and the EU Peace I Fund development officers and consultants are proactive, working hand in hand with the local community to encourage them to stimulate and develop economic projects.

Building a relationship between the IFI and EU Peace I Fund development officers and consultants and these local community group leaders is a pathway to economic regeneration of the local economy, but perhaps more importantly, a key component of local community self-efficacy and empowerment. Over the past thirty years border communities have suffered economically, politically, and psychologically from the brunt of political violence, which carved up NI's urban inner cities into sectarian enclaves and intensified the urban-rural split. In the border country of NI, Harris's (1972) study of the village of "Ballybeg" suggests that rural Protestants disliked and distrusted their political leaders in Belfast and that rural Catholic and Protestant neighbors helped each other at harvest time. Indeed, Whyte (1990) points out the heterogeneity of relationships, contacts, and experiences throughout NI society and warns against a simple rural-urban classification.

Consequently, one of the most salient themes that emerged in these interviews about the economic and political role of the IFI and the EU Peace I Fund, and the experience of dealing with both funding agencies for all local community group leaders, was their positive or negative perceptions toward the organization and its personnel, which took on an almost rural-urban fissure. For example, pro-funding agency responses around the border area range from "works closely with local communities," and "the process is much more flexible" to "has empowered local groups by restoring their pride." These descriptions of the positive effect of the funding agencies are put forth matter-of-factly and describe a win-win position of the agencies' involvement in local economic development. In contrast, antifunding agency responses from community group leaders range from "the IFI wants visual projects," to "the EU is throwing money at Protestants," to "was set up to undermine the armed struggle." For example, some of these antifunding agency comments suggest that the experience of living in Derry may have impacted some of these respondents' negative perceptions of the funding agencies. In their early days, the funding agencies were accused of refurbishing banks and public buildings and not helping poor communities. This perspective may have colored these respondents' perceptions of the IFI and the EU Peace I funds.

These comments suggest that the experience of living in an urban area where information is disseminated freely may have seriously affected the respondents' images of the funding agencies, in contrast to the empathetic perceptions of rural respondents. Or it may be that these comments reflect a process whereby the funding agencies, and in particular the IFI, has deliberately set about targeting rural areas for monies rather than urban areas. Traditionally, more resources always find their way into urban rather than rural areas because of the unitary nature of both states.

Both Ireland and Britain are unitary states with a centralized bureaucracy and power structure (Chubb 1992). The nature of both political systems has shaped the center-local relationships that have developed within both political cultures. All of the civil servants, development officers, and consultants were reflective about the necessity of rationalizing the bureaucracy to stimulate economic activity in border areas. They mentioned that the funding agencies have bypassed county councils to get resources directly into the community. On the other hand, some community group leaders along the border and in Derry mentioned that the central government bureaucracy is very powerful, and its communication with local community groups is not well developed. They believe that it is important to build up the self-esteem, self-efficacy, and education of local groups so that they can manage the language of the bureaucracy to get access to funding from both agencies.

As one would surmise, the respondents in this study had mixed feelings on most of the issues. In general, they perceived that economic aid is facilitating community empowerment and development and building community self-esteem and self-efficacy. Community leaders found that the centralized bureaucracies in Belfast and Dublin had too much control over the funding process and that in both communities the economic assistance was not going into the most deprived and marginalized sectors that really needed it. Civil servants, on the other hand, believe that the aid is getting down to the grass roots, while development officers fear the consequences of the end of agency funding for local communities. There was also a perception among Protestant respondents that Catholics are receiving all of the aid, which in the future could serve to heighten Protestant hostility and alienation.

In general, most of the respondents in this study suggest that the funding agencies are making a difference in local grassroots economic and political transformation. The funding agencies seem to create an opportunity for moving the political conflict from a win-lose context to a win-win situation for these people by expanding economic resources for local communities to work for economic growth that will spill over into peace. However, a small number of these local group leaders remind us that structural changes need to be made to provide an equal and safe context for all people in Northern Ireland to live together in a harmonious manner.

CONCLUSIONS

The end of the Cold War ignited local and exclusive ethnic loyalties in Africa, Latin America, and the former Soviet Union where poor economic conditions have escalated ethnopolitical tensions, political violence, and intractable conflict (Byrne and Irvin 2000). Without effective and peaceful intervention by third parties—states, nongovernmental organizations, international nongovernmental organizations, and scholar-practitioners— some of these ethnopolitical conflicts will spiral into ultimate chaos, and the "Lebanonization" of such conflicts will prevail (Bercovitch 1996).

At the same time, other ethnopolitical conflicts have reached a zero-sum hurting stalemate level, and have de-escalated to a less destructive stage to allow a peace-building process to be put in place. Postapartheid South Africa and the 1998 GFA come to mind as examples of recent attempts to rebuild societal structures and relationships in South Africa and NI.

In the context of NI, external funding agencies such as the IFI and the EU Peace I funds must be careful not to impose an economic development model alien to its socioeconomic and cultural context that would exacerbate its economic and political problems. Instead, a community-based economic development model must reflect the worldview of that community (Lederach 1997), one that reflects the relationship between Protestants and Catholics and between both ethnoreligious groups and the British and Irish states as well as the wider European and global milieu. A sustainable economic development model must be based on cooperation not competition, empathy, and respect for all citizens instead of hatred and distrust, security, and identity needs for all through the broadening of the identity pie (Byrne 2001b). We must not encourage anarchy and the limited perception of the self as connected to one's ethnic group if we are to promote a positive, just, and holistic peace that will empower all of NI's citizens.

Economic assistance to NI has served to restructure the political culture from violence in direct support of civil society. Consequently, insecurity and fear must be transformed through a fair political process that gives voice to and encourages the participation from all citizens in the democratic process. In that way civil society can play a more proactive and empowering role for all of NI's grassroots constituents and their political representatives. The 1998 GFA approved by the May 22 "yes" vote, for example, sets out to create a new NI by setting up new political institutions and a 108-seat local assembly in Belfast, reforming the RUC and taking the paramilitary guns out of Irish politics for good.

5

Economic Assistance and People's Perceptions of Community Empowerment and Capacity Building

INTRODUCTION

THIS CHAPTER EXPLORES HOW ECONOMIC assistance has contributed to capacity building and empowerment within the Northern Ireland peace-building process. In particular, it explores how funding from the European Union Peace I Fund and the International Fund for Ireland has nurtured capacity building and grassroots empowerment in the process of building peace.

Capacity building ensures that nongovernmental organizations and international nongovernmental organizations work with the grass roots to develop needed expertise and professional capability by exchanging, sharing, and transferring knowledge (Goodhand 2006). Capacity building aims to share resources and address basic human needs, and in the process enhance the dignity and self-esteem of local people (Schirch 2004). The ultimate goal of capacity building is to assist others to empower themselves so that they in turn can assist their communities to build a better society for everyone (Lederach 2005). Symbolic and nonverbal ritual acts are key tools to empower communities and assist them in solving complex and deep-rooted conflicts that can transform identities, relationships, and worldviews—all of which are useful in the long-term work of capacity building (Schirch 2004).

Capacity building is a multidimensional and coordinated intervention that takes place in multiple sectors in society (e.g., arts, education, health care, and politics) through external assistance in the transfer of education, research, and training (Webel and Galtung 2007). NGOs and INGOs use their expertise and experience to nurture collaborative, equitable, and interactive needs-based capacity building (Jeong 2005). The overall relevance and merit of each capacity-building activity, people-to-people interaction, and joint participation is that they build bridges of cooperation and understanding that promote the common good, enabling both peace building and long-term capacity building (Sandole 2006). Effective capacity building empowers local communities by combining deadline-oriented progress with long-term objectives (Ryan 2007) and is crucial to achieving sustainable peace.

Capacity building informs the peace-building process in a postviolent conflict society by empowering the grass roots to transform their socioeconomic, cultural, political, and ecological milieus for their own well-being and the transformation of society (Mason and Meernik 2005). Capacity building empowers people to rediscover their strengths and to develop their potential by building their self-respect and self-confidence using their human and physical resources to improve the quality of their lives (Junne and Verkoren 2004). Capacity building allows NGOS and INGOs to establish local networks and to work with the people energetically, creatively, and imaginatively to build peace and a better society (Boulding 2000). Evaluation tools are critical in assessing and monitoring the impact and consequences of capacity building in the peace-building process. Pointing to best practices, tools, and frameworks, and making recommendations to policy makers, practitioners, and leaders in all sectors of society, evaluators make sure that the best possible processes are implemented complementarily in order to institutionalize conflict prevention (Kosic and Favretto 2007). Sustainable peace involves integrating vertical capacity with horizontal capacity—those who connect the highest level of negotiation with the grassroots communities with those who move across the social divides of conflict from their identity of origin to the other community and back again. This enables the web makers to weave relational webs across social spaces, creating constructive social and political change across the complex terrain of social and political geography (Lederach 2005).

The goal of peace building is to strengthen the capacity of postviolent conflict societies, transforming conflict by using nonviolent means and inclusivity to achieve sustainable human security (Byrne 2001a). Peace building focuses on a wide range of issues including: (1) humanitarian aid, (2) sustainable economic development, (3) community development, (4) reconstruction of infrastructure, (5) second-track diplomacy, (6) economic and social reconstruction, (7) governance and democratic development, (8) institutional and civil capacity building, (9) human rights, (10) personal security, (11) policy development and advocacy, (12) development of life skills, and (13) improved health care (Boyce and O'Donnell 2007). People can make a difference. Empowered grass roots can imagine and visualize peace as individuals and believe in their own personal power, effectiveness, and self-esteem as they begin to think critically about socioeconomic and political issues and to participate in socioeconomic and political activities, thereby building capacity in their communities in a "power with" interdependent partnership approach to peace building (Boulding 2000).

Structural inequalities within societies such as inequitable power relations and economic inequality require a long-term sustainable peace-building process (Jeong 2005). Such a process necessitates a comprehensive conflict analysis and resolution capacity within local and external organizations in order to influence constructive policy making and to address the root causes of conflict, thereby reducing inequalities and promoting social justice (Lyons 2005). Internal and external parties need to work together on a wide range of issues to reduce inequality and conflict at the grassroots level while supporting change at the national level on such issues as institutional and legal reform, policing, human rights, and economic development (Byrne and Keashly 2000). Better policy and practice in the area of capacity building will ultimately enhance the livelihood and security of people affected by ethnopolitical conflict (Mason and Meernik 2005). Such a process is critical to transform the dynamics of conflict and cocreate the roots of peace and enhance the capacity of civil society to effectively interface with government, donor agencies, and other strategic civil society partnerships in order to promote conflict prevention, good governance, early warning systems, reconciliation, and a gender mainstreaming that includes women and youth in peace-building initiatives (Byrne and Keashly 2000).

Peace-building initiatives and activities involve careful and participatory planning and sustained commitment by the grass roots and external donors, as well as the coordination of various intervention efforts by a plethora of peacemaking and peace-building NGOS (Goodhand 2006). Sustainable peace is characterized by the absence of direct, cultural, and structural violence, settling core issues that underlie the conflict and changing the patterns of interaction among the parties, thereby moving them from dependency and vulnerability to self-sufficiency and well-being to promote a more peaceful future and to prevent conflict from reemerging (Galtung 1996). Building a sustainable peace means repairing relationships and addressing psychological trauma as well as transforming socioeconomic and political structures and systemic roots of conflict (Byrne 2001b; Volkan 1998).

Reconciliation is a process that allows emotional rebalancing to take place between conflict parties so that together they can create a shared space to nurture and make possible such reconnections. Such reconciliation promotes a cycle of healing and respect that breaks the cycle of victimhood and shares power in a participatory process that rehumanizes the other and builds relationships across an elicitive process of ethnopolitical divisions (Ryan 2007; Senehi and Byrne 2006). Reconciliation is relationship building at the grassroots and societal levels and is the focal point for: (1) sustained dialogue to engage the sides of a conflict with each other, (2) encounter activities to express anger and loss that accompanies injustice, and (3) innovative reconciliation techniques that exist outside of mainstream politics (Lederach 1997). Reconciliation requires both structural and relational transformation and is integral to a peace-building process that involves an array of approaches, processes, and stages, all of which are necessary for transforming relationships in a peaceful and sustainable mode and forging fair and effective government and conflict analysis and resolution, processes, and systems (Webel and Galtung 2007). Reconciliation requires a change of attitudes, beliefs, emotions, goals, and patterns of behavior that have been embedded in society for many generations (Kosic and Favretto 2007) as an intricate element in the transformation of violent intercommunal conflict (Ryan 2007). How the past is acknowledged will impact the prospects of creating a future culture of peace (Rigby 2001).

It is important to deal with complex problems at all levels of human relationships (Sandole 2006), to formulate the fiscal foundations for a sustainable state and a durable peace (Boyce and O'Donnell 2007), and to create essential policy and practice changes in the interest of enhanced peace-building efforts (Boulding 2000; Goodhand 2006). Such a process entails evaluating the effect of economic assistance to discern what has worked, what has not, and how economic assistance programs can be designed to have a more positive impact (de Zeeuw and Kumar 2006). Elections alone are not enough to advance the goals of democracy and peace (Lyons 2005). Prosperity does not guarantee peace; however, a lack of economic development may lead to renewed violence (Junne and Verkoren 2004). Thus, donors face a myriad of challenges in their attempt to provide economic assistance that will stimulate economic growth and sustainable development (Hoy 1998). In NI contact and interaction are needed to build bridges among ordinary people to promote communication, confidence building, and reciprocation in order to build trust and reconciliation among the grass roots (Dixon 2007; McGarry and O'Leary 2007).

Next, I outline what the respondents found to be important in their perceptions of how funding from the EU Peace I Fund and the IFI may be nurturing capacity-building and grassroots empowerment in the peace-building process. This chapter focuses on interviewees' opinions of the contribution of both funds to the capacity-building process and the empowerment of local citizens to better their lives.

ECONOMIC REGENERATION AND COMMUNITY EMPOWERMENT AND CAPACITY BUILDING

These respondents hold mixed views regarding the role of economic assistance in developing and empowering local communities. Civil servants are more likely to believe that there is a direct relationship between community economic regeneration and the elimination of political violence. Community group leaders suggest that the legitimization of marginalized and disadvantaged communities through economic aid plays a critical role in nurturing cross-community contact and inspiring support of nonviolent resolutions of the conflict. Many community activists noted that government agencies must commit seriously if peace-building efforts to address the long-term neglect of marginalized communities are to be sustained.

A Dublin civil servant tends to perceive a more nuanced view of the necessity for local community leaders to empower their people to become involved in local community projects:

> I like to see far more realism, and community and voluntary organizations quite often have that realism themselves. You know, the more widespread they are the better. If there are one or two sorts of locals running everything, well then of course you have bad results. But if it's fairly widely and democratically constituted, then local opinions are more about what they need and what will work in their own area than mandarins coming up from Dublin.

Further, he suggests that the EU Commission put the program forward, but it was slow to get off of the ground. The IFBs have been very successful in getting into the disadvantaged and marginalized groups at the grassroots level:

> It is not that the delivery of the program suffered in any way. It did not. But the perceptions were that a lot of things might not have been too good, and that is done partly from a misconception of the measurement of progress. . . . The program was slow in getting going because while it was drawn up and approved in record speed, the implementation of it was slow. It was slow because of the devolved nature of the program and the need to bring in groups and the need to discuss with groups what they needed. The consultation with ADM, Combat Poverty, and Cooperation North went on from December 8, 1995, and the IFBs signed the Global Grants Agreement [GGA]. The GGA was their guarantee of funding, which was signed directly between the commission on the one hand and the IFBs on the other. All government was signed on to do; the only input we had was to ensure the exchequer cofunding was made available, but the IFBs had total discretion in relation to how they operated the measures, and that is how we wanted it. The IFBs were slow to gear up in terms of sorting out the areas of need that they needed to be satisfied with before they signed a legal agreement. They physically then got their offices up and running because they in each and every case felt they needed another sub-setup of what they were doing. I thought they would

be able to absorb some of it in their existing structures. . . . Now the level of commitments, which is the grant approval stage, is quite high, and by the end of this year all the existing funding will be committed. But the progress is not based on commitments, which is a measure of how well the IFBs are doing. It is based on how well the expenditure and how well the projects are doing. And given that the projects are in the slower pace than the projects are, perhaps is the greater recognition that they are the ones we should be helping. . . . The expenditure on the other measures depended on the speed of the project promoters to get up and get going and get organized and to engage in activities that drew down and that actually resulted in money being spent rather than committed. I think that there was a misconception there as to the progress and that damaged the program greatly, and it is easy looking back in retrospect except to say that the commission had been warned about it.

In his story, another civil servant in Dublin highlights the connection between economic growth and the demise of terrorism. He views economic development promoting cross-community contact reducing sectarianism in the process:

We are trying to create better economic conditions so that there is less emphasis on the violence of the process. It will not make the political settlement happen but it will mean that people on the ground are less attracted by the extreme philosophy that is on any side. So you are promoting a more fertile ground for acceptance of any settlement, promoting some kind of local stability, which will be eager to accept a political solution, which will put across NI and the border region. So that is what we are at, if you like. And we are doing that by economic regeneration and by making the two communities get to know each other better. And they will be more inclined to accept a political combination. So that would be how we would see ourselves fitting into the overall political and economic situation.

He adds:

In fact, if you speak to the program leaders in NI, most of them, a lot of them, would admit to you that at the voluntary level, they were into more single-identity projects than they would have liked, because that was the way they had to go. But the effort was maintained and the pressure was made to try and keep in the cross-community as best they could, and they would build some of the projects. In the long term you get a project based on single identity (within one community) whereas phase two will be based on cross-community contact. That way, you have got a cross-community project that doesn't involve any cross-community work for a year or two and that moves on.

A development officer with the EU Peace I Fund in Co. Tyrone argues that many community-based projects will fold after all of the external funding is gone. He also thinks that there is a perception in Derry within the Protestant community that the money is going strictly into the Catholic community:

You can see it very much in Derry. There is a theory for the reason why. Derry is booming because for so long people in Derry community groups never got anything from the district councils, because there had been sectarian barriers up, and now they actually are able to tap into funds and capital funds. You know, they have said, "We are going to do it ourselves." There is a sort of entrepreneurial self-help spirit almost there. "We are no eejits. We will do it ourselves." That's just a theory. But I think there is a certain amount of truth in it. We have just got to go and do it. Like the opposite of being Protestant. They have been very much, always been given work in particular, and then in the 1960s, then 1970s, then 1980s, suddenly there is no work, there is no handouts. There is no "Send me Jimmy down in the morning, and I will give him a job down in the shipyard." It stopped overnight, not overnight. It stopped through the industrialization of Britain in general, and you are now seeing a wee bit of a fight back. But there is a Protestant-Catholic perception, especially in rural development, problems with Protestant groups who perceive money going to Catholic community groups. I mean, that is sold very well. I'm sure you are well aware of [this], but you know, the perception. The perception is [there], and I think there is a bit more truth in it than the perception that the Catholic community, because there is a community spirit, the Catholic areas as compared to the Protestant areas, are classed more as self-help or "do your own thing" and don't rely on other people.

The IFBs are able to get right down to the grassroots level, according to a community group leader from Co. Monaghan. However, there is tension between statutory agencies and IFBs. Power is at the center in Dublin and elected members of the government are afraid of giving that power to local community groups and to IFBs in the voluntary sector that are distributing funds to these local community groups. He goes on to say that representatives of partnership boards in the Republic of Ireland wouldn't be responsible to the electorate in the same way that elected politicians are, and that could be a political problem down the road:

There are partnership boards which we have established in each county and a Strategy Committee, but that is not finding favor with the elected representatives, because they are saying, "Why should these guys who don't offer themselves for election, why should these fellas have an equal right with us who had to offer ourselves to the electorate?" That is very strong among the county council members, because the state is saying to them, "You sit down in partnership with these community groups," and they say, "Why should we?" and the emphasis, I have to say, is on that. The emphasis in Brussels seems to be very strongly behind that concept of partnerships, between local communities and elected representatives. Then elected representatives should move on a bit. In fact, I had a conference a couple of weeks ago on that very same theme, and they were all very much against partnerships. Partnerships should be there. But they should be subservient to the electoral process, they shouldn't be shared. . . . This partnership principle is operated far more through the North of Ireland, and these partnership boards are getting a tremendous amount of peace money to administer in the North. . . . You see, I do believe that would happen with partnerships, that you have democracy without responsibility, so that is fine, and it is great to involve people, but at the end of the day, the elected fellow has to be responsible. He is answerable. The partnerships are not answerable to anybody except themselves, and that is what I would find, as I say, wrong with them.

A community leader from Derry believes that sustainable economic development that psychologically empowers both communities can radically enhance their quality of life. This is what he had to say on this issue:

Economic development, I think, is really important in that it would give a lot of people the possibility of getting jobs. The possibility of wealth creation is really important for almost all of us in our lives. We recognize that. The second parallel depends on the quality of the economic development. If it is an economic development of the type that says we can do basic poor work for poor wages, then it is another way of treating us bad. It is enculturalization.

In contrast, an IFI consultant and development officer in the border region outlines how the Troubles psychologically and economically impacted border communities. Moreover, he discusses how IFI funding has rekindled the self-esteem and self-efficacy of border communities by delivering economic assistance into deprived areas. He supports the idea about the proactive role of IFI in building the peace process:

On the one hand, you have got the deprivation, let's say in the rural areas that I deal with. You talk about small farm structure, high-age profile in the population and high emigration. In the Southern border counties, falling populations and failure to adapt to agricultural change are problems. So there is a whole set of circumstances that leads to economic stagnation, regressive poor demography, and on top of that and mixed in with that, you have the impact of the Troubles in divided communities in just the threat of violence being there causing a difficult operating environment. And I think that was very much the case during the late 1970s and the early 1980s saying [in] the border counties that the threat of violence was always there. There was the symbolic closure of the border roads, but always the physical disruption was a major inhibitor to trade in towns that would have been under stress anyway even if they would have been placed in Munster, for example. Like places that we were talking about earlier, such as Belturbet, Killeshandra, and Clones, all of those towns needed to change anyway to keep pace with the changes in society and the changes in the economy. . . . Sligo, for example, is not a county that touches the border, but talking with people, say, in the retail trade in Sligo, they will say, for example, "We had a bomb scare in Sligo yesterday which brought the town to a standstill for about two or three hours" . . . The IFI has helped to raise confidence levels of that and has helped enormously to stimulate private investment. A bit of public investment in the border towns will very quickly trigger, say closed-down retail premises might be reevaluated because they were refurbished and looked all right and looked good and fit in with the rest of the street and maybe there is a bit of life here after all. It has helped the level of optimism. There has been a huge amount of community empowerment that has taken place as a result of the funds' activities, which I think has been very positive and has brought in a new confidence to people in the area. It has helped to defuse a lot of suspicions of the cross-border activities. . . . It is difficult to separate the two sets of influence. On the one hand, there are the normal causes of factors in deprivation and disadvantage, and regret in a lot of cases and the Troubles. I do think the normal situation or disadvantage that has existed in the border counties has been greatly exaggerated by the Troubles. It is probably most clearly evident in the area of tourism where people have this perception that it is not a safe place to go and that has certainly measured the impact on all of the areas that I would deal with. . . . It has helped the level of optimism.

In contrast, a community group leader in Co. Monaghan believes that the political conflict has socialized both communities to think in a certain manner about the border between Northern and Southern Ireland. Further, he maintains that there is little commitment from the civil servants in Belfast and Dublin to market the border area to tourists and business interests:

I think that if there is not commitment at the top level, for example, Bord Failte or the Tourism Department within the government, then investment is pointless. You could go and pour endless millions of pounds into the whole border regions but if the commitment is not there to send people out you know, it's irrelevant. And if they do not work with community groups on the ground, that is where it is going to be built from. It is normally built from the top down. It has to be built from the ground up, not from the top down.

In addition, a community leader from Co. Cavan suggests that local people are empowering their communities and in the process bypassing local county councillors who perceive that their power base is threatened. His comments illustrate how international funding blurs the boundaries between local and state governments:

> I can see that local county councillors don't know where they stand at the present time because they seem to have lost their bit of ground, and groups like us have taken over from them, and we are doing our own thing. We are no longer going to those people and trying to push them to do something for us. We are able to do it for ourselves at the present time.

Moreover, another community leader from Co. Monaghan expresses positive social norms that both IFI and EU Peace I development officers have played an important role in highlighting the needs of the local communities they are serving:

> I would think a lot would go back to the original thing of removing a lot of layers of the bureaucracy. As far as I would see it now, I think both Mr. X of IFI and Mr. Y of EU Peace and Reconciliation would come out and talk to a group. They are in touch with a group and know what is going on.

Yet, another community group leader in Co. Monaghan maintains that a new sustainable economic development process that cements IFI and the EU Peace I development consultants is working with local people in the grass roots. He recognizes that his community members are impoverished, cynical, and agitated if they perceive that nothing constructive is occurring to empower their communities:

> Community development is a much slower process than most people think. That's the major thing that we are talking about with community development. And we need a much longer process of support with quality people, quality development officers, working with people on the ground. That is a major, major priority, and if that is not tackled then the last date is worse than the first. And what you're left with is a group of people whose hopes you have raised. And most people in rural Ireland, they got so much of that. They are pretty cynical about it. And the biggest breakthrough that you have to make is to get people to say it's another load of rubbish. We have heard it all before. And the danger is that they will have heard it all before. And the funds will dry up again and the people will pull out. You will have left the people more disenchanted and disillusioned than before, and if that happens, the last date is worse than the first.

Interestingly, a community group leader from Co. Cavan indicates that intragroup conflict within community groups is not uncommon. For example, in his community group in Belturbet, the conflict lines are centered on the age variable. The core members of the group are the retired and experienced professionals, while the young professionals are not proactively engaged in regenerating their community:

> Well you see the peculiarity of something like this in that people are inclined to be a bit different, about a community like this. The generality of people in small communities is that they tend to be conservative. They tend to resent change. It is a natural human condition, and traditionally we in this community, we're a sort of, the business people here, we're of the older age group and they tended to be a little bit conservative. Now we have a younger business community, a younger vintage, people who are well educated, people who have gone through the educational system, and the strange thing about it is that the older people were far more venturesome. The younger people wouldn't want to touch this with a barge pole. The executives who are pushing this project here are largely people like myself who are retired, and the younger people are far more conservative than their older counterparts. They don't want to get involved at all because there is nothing in it for them. They feel there is a risk in this and it might cost them money. I feel the executives feel that if this thing is up and running and shown to be a success, well then these young people will probably take a better interest in it. It is easier to get part and parcel of something that is successful than to get at the cold face and actually work. But this is one thing that we have noticed, that the younger people have never even come down near it. You have a vibrant and younger quite successful business people and they don't get involved at all in the community at any meaningful level which I find unusual. . . . I don't know whether there is any reason for it. I can't really understand it because the general critique of the business people here was that they were better off and didn't really care. But when we went around the town looking for support, it was the older people who handed us out the money and the younger people didn't. There were a few exceptions, of course. There is one person in particular in the town, who is actually retired from business, [who] wrote us out a check for a thousand pounds, never asked "Yes, Aye, or No."

He adds that the funding agencies have given heart back to local communities by restoring their pride and belief in a future. Furthermore, he argues that if people have a fair chance to prosper, then they won't destroy their milieu:

> At the end of the day a lot of conflict is predicated by disadvantage, unemployed people in ghetto areas who can see no future. And, for instance, a project like this couldn't actually be undertaken without the assistance of the funding agencies, and the very fact that they were there gave the community here the courage to do what they are doing. It wouldn't be

physically possible to do it. It wouldn't be physically possible to put the physical structures in place. It wouldn't be physically possible to develop them. I think there is a great future for this area. There is a great future for this country. When people get an economic stake, they are less likely to destroy it. I mean once an economic level of sustenance is reached, people have a stake. They are less inclined to involve themselves in conflict at a communal or other level. Revolution occurs in poor societies. They rarely occur in prosperous societies. I don't know if I'm right in that generalization or not, but I would believe that. You may have minor ripples, but you rarely have revolutions in prosperous societies. I mean that is predicated by the fact now there is a level of distribution. Where people have a stake, an economic stake in the community, they are less inclined to destroy it. Economic inclusion and total inclusion and the conflict in the North of Ireland are as a result of the perception of people, perceiving that they were outside of the mainstream. For instance, a large section of the population of NI felt that they had no say in how they were being governed. The fact that they had no say in how they were being governed, whether that is right or wrong, that was the perception. If people can feel that they are part and parcel of how they are being governed and feel that they are generally getting a fair crack of the whip, and again that they get the economic injection to help themselves then they wont resort to violence and revolt. For instance, if I build a little wall down in my garden and spend the money on it, I get a sense of satisfaction. I'm not inclined to back the tractor in on it and toss it down again.

Similarly, a community group leader from Co. Monaghan makes the point that a new long-term economic development process is needed with IFI development consultants working with local people on the ground. He understands that people who are impoverished in his community are cynical and get annoyed if they perceive that nothing is happening. This is what he had to say:

What I am saying is that the effectiveness of the process will require much longer-term help than is being thought of at present. Say peace and reconciliation was being talked about for two or three years . . . how do you develop a group of people—maybe ten, fifteen, twenty people—and get them to analyze their own area, to do up with the needs of their own area, to train themselves to implement it and to see it through, and to stay with a project to see it through. You can't do that.

Moreover, a community group leader from Co. Fermanagh suggests that some groups believe that "peace is a business" and that the money is not targeted to the disadvantaged areas that really need it. The Catholic community was always proactive, organized, and knew how to organize around the resources, whereas Protestants did not have the same experience to organize together in community groups to apply for funds:

There is a great danger in trying to form a community for the sake of drawing down money, or because there is money there to draw. This is a very weak basis for forming a community. Now the Catholic communities, they did not derive this expertise overnight. They have had it there for a long time, long before this money was available. They had fund-raising organizations in various sports organizations and all their schools. So, there was a culture there of community activism. There is a religious element in it because it is not about religion. It is not about Catholics fighting Protestants. But there is an overarching religious element of the Catholic ethos and the Protestant ethos, and I am not talking about Ireland even. I am talking about Europe in general. The Protestant ethos is about "me myself," the Catholic ethos is about community, and the Protestant ethos is about making money. I am not saying that Catholics do not want to make money. This is purely an observation. Anyone listening to me in NI would say it is a dinosaur observation coming from a Catholic. But I see this as, there is a cultural background of Catholic culture, quite apart from NI altogether. . . . I am not sure that this is where I disagree with the guy from the EU. You can't throw money at a problem and hope to resolve it. To my mind in fact, and I said this two to three years ago when the fund was launched, the Peace and Reconciliation fund, I said it in Belfast, that if the money had been put into a trust fund it would have been far more usefully spent because it would have been there for generations. The single biggest scourge, and this is not a personal view, everybody you meet says it, was this unholy haste to get the money spent, for budgetary reasons or for whatever it is. And if you are not seen to be spending the money, you don't want it and therefore you will lose it. So get the money spent. Get it out. It has in many instances been very foolishly spent, not because of any wrong motive but because of an unholy pressure to get the applications in, get them processed. I know I have been through the whole thing, without sufficient time to think.

Similarly, another community group leader from Co. Fermanagh feels that Unionists are afraid of change and feel that all the external funding is going to the Catholic community. Protestants were traumatized by Catholic actions in the 1960s. Now Protestants perceive that the external monies to the Catholic community are unfair and unjust:

This has annoyed Protestant businessmen and Protestants generally so they see this, they don't like this. "Where are the Catholics getting the money?" And of course they have good reason to say, "Well, let's look at this situation, and the situation needs looking at, and it needs explaining and pulled out in the open, and we all need to look at the situation." So, we had a meeting of Protestant businessmen about eighteen months to a year ago who were very concerned that the money was going in the Catholic direction not in the Protestant direction, so we have this problem. If you are going to look from the outside at the problem, you are going to say

"Let's increase Catholic employment, and that is going to increase Protestant disquiet at the same time." . . . We need to deal with the perceptions of the Protestants, and in fact giving out the money might be perfectly just and reasonable. The perception on the Protestant side is that it is not just and reasonable. So what I am saying is the Catholics are coming up and looking for things for all sorts of reasons. They are the ones who are looking, partially because of need, and partially because they are organized for doing this. The Protestants are on the ball as much for looking and there is one reason for that at the moment, and there we see Catholics are not exported in the ways of the past.

A number of community group leaders in Derry suggest that even though there are problems accessing funds, the IFI and the EU Peace I Fund are important catalysts in promoting social change within the Nationalist community. Community group access to the funding agencies is limited, according to one of these community group leaders. He suggests that the EU Peace I Fund is well advertised, but the IFI is difficult to get hold of:

I suppose the wherewithal to follow through leads to access to the funding, and we would generally have a collective ability to prepare applications and so on. However, there are many other groups on the ground that don't have those resources available to them. Our function is to be the base for the local partnership to ensure that local groups on the ground are serviced with that information and we like to think that we have some success in that respect. Then the other local communities are not as well organized as our own. And the special support program to some extent and certainly very, very many IFBs appeal to reach out and link into those communities. . . . The proposal has accelerated its development within the past year, and we have found that the IFI has been more amenable and more available to us in terms of helping to negotiate options for the funding of this scheme. That has been linked into extensive lobbying through the Department of Foreign Affairs in Dublin, and also through the U.S. Congress and a number of other range of people within and on the periphery of the Irish diaspora in the U.S. That has had a significant effect upon the facilities and the assistance afforded to us.

There is an impossible mix of criteria that makes it difficult for groups to apply for funding because they may not be in a position to make the group composition and project cross-community. People who work in other community neighborhoods can be shot by paramilitaries. Individuals from the other community can also include their name in support of the other community's application grant without the project being a real cross-community reconciliation process. Another community group leader in Derry thinks that the IFI wants visual projects:

The IFI tend to look at grant aid of ten and twenty thousand pounds, but it really is something that [they] can't bring American visitors to see. They like to bring them to big projects, like the Raphaoe Center at Creggan. I am not arguing with that, but that is the type of project they can bring visitors to say, "This is where your money went," instead of bringing them to Rosemount and saying, "Well, there is a girl working. She is not in at the minute, and you are helping to pay her wages." What has she actually done? How do you show that a woman in a house has become more than a mother, and a wife, that her attitudes have changed a bit? How do you show that? That somebody has stopped drinking, or how do you show that some kid has stopped taking E's? It is difficult to quantify those sort of things, and Americans, I think there is a feeling within the people involved with the IFI that they want visual projects that they can point to, to the funders. I don't know if that is coming because of pressure from America which says, "If we give you money, we want to see the results," or whether it is people here saying, "we got money from America, and we want to show them results." I don't know who is responsible for that.

Another group leader from Derry maintains that the IFI is now throwing money at Protestant community projects. Protestant groups did not accept IFI money in the past. It is difficult to get Protestants to join cross-community groups:

There is a Learning Center up there, who got a grant of four hundred thousand pounds, to do with arts and learning. They got four hundred thousand pounds from the IFI for a project because they had to be seen giving to Protestants because Protestants had refused to take IFI money and said it was blood money. Now they are beginning to warm to it. Now they are shoveling money in that direction. I have a program funded by IFI and that is the one. They funded the thing in South Africa and Southern Florida. They will only fund that thing in South Africa if I can get my act together. You are talking about serious money here. In our present program between Leitrim and ourselves, that's the Catholic and Protestant one, it is always easier to get Catholics in the South. You might get some Protestants in the North, but it always ends up that there is a minority of Protestants on it.

He goes on to question why some of the projects that do indeed fill a community need are not funded, in particular, by the EU Peace I Fund. This is what he had to say:

I'm surprised at the nature of some of the ones that have got programs and things that are meant to do with the university. They will have got money. There are people getting money at the minute, which I have great difficulty with. For instance, I think universities should be funded out of government funds. The university should not be entitled to it. I'll tell you what I did, because of the nature of this organization. I was very careful not to hit the big money. I would look for small money. This is a simple one. I am building twenty-eight small units for accommodation to accommodate homeless people. All I asked from the EU Fund was, "Please give me enough money to furnish them." I was turned down and I don't know why. You could say to yourself that it fits every criterion that they could ever think of, because I was dealing with drug addicts who wouldn't build normal homes, and these special needs. Drug addicts, alcoholics, and it was a kind of almost transitional housing in a way, that you take them off the street, put them in there. You give them a living room, a sitting room, a kitchen, a small bathroom. They have the dignity of having their own key to the door. There is a warden onsite, and if there is a problem, they get access to therapists. They have access to someone who will teach them to cook, someone helping them to make up their budget or whatever, and this is a beautiful program. All I asked was "Please furnish the flats for me at maybe three hundred pounds a flat." That was all I needed.

According to another community group leader from Derry, the IFI was set up as part of both governments' political agendas to undermine the Republican armed struggle and was used for the British government's projects, not for local community socioeconomic development. He also argues that the IFI now targets deprivation in local areas:

The reason the IFI was originally set up was when the British government, then under the auspices of Margaret Thatcher, the then prime minister, and Garreth FitzGerald, who was Taoiseach [prime minister] in the South, and Ronald Reagan who was then the president of the U.S. People who would not in my view be people who would be very happy with the notion of community employment and social ownership, and cooperatives, and employee ownership, and so forth. This fund was originally set up to put a focus on Ireland in terms of the need to build up the economic infrastructure, particularly in the North and the border counties of Ireland. But all people felt there was a political agenda there, and part of the political agenda there was to undermine the armed struggle. Now clearly when that particular process began, lots of groups on the ground required money and required resources. As an organization, we sought information about the IFI and it would be fair to say in its very first year, there was major controversy because the money that American taxpayers and other people throughout Europe were prepared to give us for all the right reasons, to put investment into Ireland. They might not have considered maybe some of the wider political undertones of why it was set up in the first place. They genuinely thought they were helping. The money was not hitting areas of disadvantage, and one of the things that Northern Ireland Co-operative Development Agency (NICDA) and a number of community organizations that I was involved in at that time, was that we assisted in making a television program about the diversion of funds from the IFI and that it was being used for pet projects of the British government at that time. It was going to private sector organizations. We felt that this money should have been going to organizations including those in greatest need, and as a result of that there was a change of policy and a change of chairmanship. I am not saying it was because of that program. I think there was lots of concern that the money wasn't filtering down. Now as a result of that shift I actually believe that the IFI has been one of the most important catalysts for bringing about social change within the areas of disadvantage, both within Catholic and Protestant working-class areas. I think that change came through the new chair that came in who had a different approach to the first chair. The current chair is a man called Mr. William McCarter who is chair of the Fruit of the Loom company. He is from Donegal and he also has factories here in the North. I think he has also been of immense benefit to assisting community economic regeneration. A man who comes from a Protestant background, and he is obviously taking a risk on a number of projects that I know NICDA is now involved in, and have been funded. The first funding mechanism was the IFI, which then brought the Department of the Environment into play, and then they became engaged in local areas, so that we would be developing relationships with key policy makers within those organizations. I think the IFI was the key. The money could have been put into a trust fund and let out over future years because we are not going to resolve this thing in two or three years. If that money was put into a trust fund, it could have been there for twenty-five years, and a lot better use put to it.

In addition, another community group leader from Derry thinks that IFI capital projects entice applications from community groups who have more of an economic focus. This is what he had to say on the issue:

I suppose there are many groups. The one good thing about Ireland in general is that there is a really vibrant community politics. Community action, I think, is quite developed in comparison to other countries, and maybe that is a reflection of the sort of the political depth of it, so much as they are open to the conflict especially in the North. So, I suppose there is a diversity of groups, and there are also a lot of groups that will spring up around single issues, and so on, and all of those groups have sought funds from the peace package. I mean, particularly from the peace package not so much from IFI. I think that IFI attracts a certain type of group, a group that is at a certain level of development, and obviously those that have an economic slant to what they are doing. Many groups, say who are into minority issues, would not be interested in economic development, and whereas, IFI would be very much focused on that. So a lot of IFI projects would be around, say rural areas and sort of urban areas that are quite depressed, sort of the major capital projects. The variety and the type of project, I think, has given the peace package something of a headache, and when they come to evaluate, and then obviously have some kind of evaluation, when they come to evaluate IFI and its impact, it will be quite interesting. The projects are quite diverse, but maybe that is a good thing. It is not necessarily a bad thing, but no doubt, it is going to get more complex.

A Derry community group leader strongly supports the fact that economic development gives a job and self-esteem to people in local communities. Economic development must not mean creating low-paying, unimportant jobs or that will damage the self-confidence of the people beyond repair:

> I think there are very clear links given the whole basis of Western civilization, which says that your value, your worth is on what you do, what job you have, whether you are president of the United States, a plumber, or whatever, that is how we value you. And if you are unemployed, and if your father before you is unemployed, you are not worth very much is the message that you get every day. And if that box in the corner is saying to you to be a truly valuable member of society, you must have Nike or you must have whatever it is that is the latest consumer product, and if your children are receiving that message and you can't deliver that, you are feeling worse and worse about yourself. And you end up in the age-old trap of drinking too much, smoking too much, trying to find some ways of using drugs to offer you a way out. It is like the North American Indian. You get trapped into a sense of trying to meet the demand of a value system that is entirely foreign to them, to their nature and their well-being, and they can't cope with it. Now, I don't think that a lot of those value systems are entirely foreign to us. We have become quite adaptable and quite adapted to all of that. As a small island on the margins of Europe and so on, we have a great potential for creativity and a very young population and quite youthful ideas and a readiness to change and be flexible and face down anything. We have all that going for us. We have a diaspora of people, many of whom would love to come home and energize the place.

Yet, another community group leader from Derry believes that economic development has helped to shape a new society by targeting economic inequality and neglect. However, the focus of the economic restructuring must be on the "single identity" of each community. Because of the siege mentality within the Unionist community, the Nationalist and the Unionist communities must first develop to meet their own economic needs before they can eventually work together:

> There seems to be three questions in there and I will try and deal with them in the order that I would prefer. Yes, economic development, economic assistance is crucial to work on the ground and the reconstruction of this society. . . . In regard to the third point you made as to whether

economic development had a role to play in a cross-community basis, yes it does. But the reality is an underage society, and while our experience has been one of seeking to mark out joint territories where we can collaborate with the English community on economic development projects, there is an acknowledged and admitted resistance within the Unionist community to reciprocate in certain ways and the concept of the siege mentality, therefore, is not appreciated. It is a very real and a very vivid experience within Unionism, and for the Unionist community, and that creates barricades or blocks for themselves to actually work in economic terms on a cross-community basis. I know there are exceptions to that rule in some parts of Belfast and elsewhere.

Similarly, yet another community group leader in Derry is of the opinion that economic assistance should be allocated to empower both working-class communities. This is what he had to say on the issue:

External funding should actually be concentrating on inequality within the society. That does not mean that all of the money should go to the Nationalist community, but it would by definition mean that money would be going to empower working-class communities and to let those communities set their own agenda in terms of what they think they need, and that agenda should not be set by the Peace and Reconciliation industry within the North.

Further, another community group leader in Derry believes that the money has raised people's expectations in the short term, and he considers what happens when the money flow is cut off. He believes contentious political issues have to be addressed before real reconciliation can take place between both communities. Moreover, he thinks that the development of economic projects will give each community confidence in its own ability to harness its energy to reach across the sectarian divide:

I have to say it has made a difference. It has made a difference of—there are two sides to this—giving us resources that we didn't have. We have people working who wouldn't be working without this money. There is a potential that some of the projects will have long-term benefits. The problem I think is that it has raised expectations, and those expectations are not being met. In the longer term, it could create a real serious anticlimax, where peoples' jobs finally run out. The project hasn't had sufficient time to develop to the level it should have. It maybe didn't get the funding or support it needed. It got some, and the project has half kicked off. People have seen the goal just ahead of them and just can't reach it. That would create real problems here. Now it has created in the short term some benefits, but it will create long-term problems unless they are backed up and supported and given support on that level. The terms and conditions of

Peace and Reconciliation, anything would allow people to develop their own projects, which allows them to understand, which gives them a job, is a step toward peace. Reconciliation, I think, is a broader issue. I think that reconciliation can only go to a certain level and the broader issues aren't involved.

In summary, some of our respondents are enthusiastic supporters of the funding process, while others perceive that local communities are not empowered economically. These responses illustrate that the respondents are divided about whether external economic funding has assisted local communities to economically regenerate themselves.

DISCUSSION

This chapter has explored respondents' perceptions of economic assistance from the IFI and the EU Peace I funds with regard to community empowerment and capacity building in NI. Ordinary men and women can make a difference working for peace locally in transforming civil society (Van Tongeren, Hellema, and Verhoeven 2005). Transforming and empowering individuals at the microlevel is a critical ingredient of grassroots peace building (Ryan 2007; Gurtov 2007).

Four main conclusions flow from this analysis. First, some respondents were of the opinion that both funders are providing the resources to empower local communities. Community and voluntary organizations promote contact, cooperation, and positive attitudes among the participants that prevent violence. In addition, the Intermediary Funding Bodies created by the EU Commission are successful in bringing Catholics and Protestants together to break down barriers as they work together to fund local community projects, which involves a lot of consultation with community and voluntary organizations. In particular, the funds have encouraged the development of a new confidence and optimism among border communities who stagnated as a result of emigration, the Troubles, and the decline of agriculture and tourism. Funding agency development officers who hail from the local milieu are empowering local community groups as they steer their projects through the complexity of the application process and discuss the projects in great detail with the community group in question. Both funders have given local communities a "fair crack of the whip," the courage to start new projects, and to include those on the margins of society. Once the individuals have an economic stake in the community, they are less likely to destroy it. The available resources have nurtured the entrepreneurial self-help spirit of the Catholic community to be creative in starting development projects themselves. The Catholic community's cultural ethos and activism is to work for the Catholic community in contrast to the focus on self within the Protestant community.

Second, other respondents argued that both funding agencies were in fact disempowering local communities. A power struggle exists between county and district councils and the IFBs. Both sets of councils dislike the partnerships with local communities and perceive voluntary groups as usurping their political power. Councillors answer to the electorate in contrast to community organizations with the result that democracy exists without responsibility. In addition, a perception exists that the funding is creating menial employment opportunities, co-opting rather than empowering the grass roots. There is also a perception within the Protestant community that IFI and EU Peace I resources are going directly into the Catholic community. Both funders are perceived as unjust. This perception existed within rural and urban Protestant communities, indicating Protestant suspicions of the intentions of both funds and both governments.

Third, some respondents suggested that the funding was encouraging capacity building to take place within the grass roots. The idea that Peace I is encouraging single-identity projects so that each community can build up its own capacity was evident in urban areas. The focus of the Peace II Fund then will highlight cross-community contact to reduce sectarianism and build bridges of reconciliation. Some respondents were of the opinion that the IFI was established in 1985 to undermine the Republican armed struggle, not to encourage social partnerships and community employment. Thus, they perceived the current change in direction of IFI policy from funding British government projects to promoting social change within disadvantaged areas and community economic regeneration as a positive development. Others averred that the funding is building the self-esteem of the community—psychological empowerment—by providing meaningful employment opportunities for a creative and youthful workforce. The dignity of having a meaningful job assists young people to break out of the cycle of depression and drug and alcohol abuse. These young people have hope and a future. Other respondents suggested that the funding also assists in reconstructing and reshaping society initially on a single-identity basis due to the siege mentality and resistance to change within the Protestant community. They argue that the funding must empower working-class communities to map out their own agenda, which is not set by the Peace and Reconciliation bureaucracy. Single-identity projects energize and instill confidence within each community as it taps into its own abilities and meets its own expectations over the long term. They argued that anything that gives local people a meaningful job is a step toward peace. They also warned that long-term economic problems will continue to exist unabated if the funding is not sustained.

Fourth, other respondents were of the opinion that the funding was not nurturing capacity building to take place within local communities. Inter-generational group conflict within rural conservative communities who resent change pitted the older entrepreneurial businesspeople against the young, vibrant, and educated business class. The latter were not willing to take the risk of starting something new for the good of the whole community. This group also perceived that long-term development will not occur because the funding will eventually end. Local projects are going to need funding assistance for fifteen to twenty years for those projects to be effective, significant, and sustainable. The majority of groups on the ground do not have the resources or expertise to complete the funders' application forms. The criteria ensure that the application process is near to impossible to meet because it is difficult to put together a tangible cross-community project. In addition, there was a perception that large visual projects were more significant for the IFI than funding a plethora of smaller local projects where the real development of people is taking place. Moreover, the perception is that the IFI is funding bizarre projects within the Protestant community as it needs to be seen to be funding projects emanating from that ethnoreligious group. In the past Protestants rejected the IFI because they perceived that the fund was part of an Irish American plot to drive NI out of the Union. These respondents also found it perplexing that the EU Peace I Fund was funding University of Ulster and Queen's University of Belfast projects, and not local community initiatives that meet a real need. Also, the complexity of different groups in terms of philosophical ethos, focused agenda, and the plethora of issues they address will make it extremely difficult for the funders to evaluate their impact in terms of sustainable development, building cross-community ties, reconciliation, and in terms of the overall impact of the funders to the NI peace process.

CONCLUSIONS

I hope that this chapter has shown a clear understanding of the perils, pitfalls, and successes of the IFI and EU Peace I funds in terms of capacity building at the grassroots level. These findings are mixed. Some of the respondents were of the opinion that the economic assistance is empowering local communities to build their capacities. Others have argued that the funds were in fact disempowering local communities and not building up their capacities. Economic assistance is not a panacea to transform relationships and structures within NI but it can be an integral part of a multitrack peace-building process to promote positive and improved intergroup attitudes and relationships, to build trust, and to change mind-sets and transform structures to promote a shared civic culture (McGarry and O'Leary 2007). Building a stable peace takes time and patience and must address all of the specific issues that underlie the conflict as a whole (Hauss 2001).

6

Economic Assistance and People's Perceptions of Reconciliation and Cross-Community Relationships

INTRODUCTION

THIS CHAPTER EXPLORES THE ROLE OF EXTERNAL economic aid as an attempt to build the peace dividend and promote reconciliation between perceived Protestant Unionists and Catholic Nationalists within the protracted intercommunal conflict in Northern Ireland. Specifically, it analyzes how external funding from the European Union Peace and Reconciliation or Peace I Fund and the International Fund for Ireland may play an important political and economic role in promoting cross-cultural contact and reconciliation between the perceived Protestant and Catholic communities in NI, and between the communities on both sides of the Irish border. External economic aid may also help build peace between both communities by sustaining contact through joint-venture economic projects at the grassroots level. Further, this chapter proposes that in order to change subjective criteria such as misperceptions, fear, and prejudice, it is necessary to promote socioeconomic contact by focusing local community attention on the promotion of superordinate goals (Sandole 1999). To help societies recover from historical violent trauma, it is necessary for economic cooperation to spill over into the political and cultural arenas to de-escalate the intensity of protracted ethnonational conflict (Pearson 2001).

The socioeconomic tensions of the 1990s, in the form of poverty, deprivation, and the inclusion of the socially excluded, provided a new psychological boost to community economic development and the idea of social economy (Tomlinson 1995). The unemployment rate has continued to rise in NI as agriculture and manufacturing have diminished (Byrne and Ayulo 1998). Consequently, the significance of community socioeconomic and political development is more essential to the communities of NI because the political and socioeconomic tensions combined are very likely to escalate into political violence (Irvin and Byrne 2002). Thus, a holistic and organic peace-building process must synergize an interactive dynamic interplay of both socioeconomic development and conflict resolution. This synthesis of views on economic aid to NI represents a significant contribution to contemporary knowledge about the merging of development and conflict resolution when applied to the protracted conflict.

John Burton's (1990) human needs theory and John Paul Lederach's (1997) conceptual framework for peace building provide the strategic link between local economic development and conflict resolution. Human needs theory provides an analytical problem-solving approach as an important conflict resolution tool and as a conceptual framework for organizing economic development initiatives at the grassroots level (Burton 1990). In addition, the linkages between economic aid, conflict resolution, and peace building ensures that constructive conflict transformation involves a partnership between local communities, governments, and nongovernmental organizations to create funding categories that are related to a new vision of thinking and peace building (Lederach 1997).

The provision of resources for transforming protracted conflict is not a matter of giving money to local community groups. A new commitment combined with creative ways of thinking about the various categories of activity, as well as the accountability and responsibility for their implication, are critical ingredients of a proactive peace-building process (Lederach 1997, 93). Economic development initiatives and conflict resolution frameworks are, thus, inextricably intertwined within local grassroots communities. NGOs and governments are both organized and empowered in an organic and holistic fashion to think about social needs and proactively engage processes that pragmatically address the larger structural dimensions of conflict. An organic process involves people in a web of activities across all levels of society (ibid., 39).

Social change demands that communities provide a comprehensive approach that emphasizes socioeconomic, psychological, and spiritual processes of transformation necessary to sustain the vision of where those processes are going (Lederach 1995). Local eclectic models of response to conflict are important because external solutions cannot be parachuted into different cultural contexts (Lederach 1997, 35). Structural peace building necessitates the creation of action thinking and institutional structures that help build a culture of peace (Diamond and McDonald 1996). Socioeconomic, psychocultural, and political infrastructures built around an organic notion of what "peace is" will provide avenues to realistically transform conflict and foster reconciliation (Byrne, Sandole, Sandole-Staroste, and Senehi 2008).

Economic aid has become an institutionalized mechanism of attempting to resolve conflict at the international level (Hampson 1996). Before the 1989 collapse of the Berlin wall, economic aid was an instrument of realpolitik—keeping allies within each superpower's sphere of influence. The New World Order, however, changed the nature of the United States' role in global economic development (Agnew and Corbridge 1994). Aid reorientation was complicated by a Republican-dominated Congress, budgetary strains, and aid fatigue (Grant and Nijman 1998, 8). The United States now uses economic aid as an indication of its support for legitimate governments that promote Western liberal democratic values (Agnew and Corbridge 1994; Grant and Nijman 1998). Consequently, both the IFI and the EU Peace I funds have linked economic aid to political progress in the peace process in NI.

Lederach (1997) warns against hurling economic aid at intricate and complex internal political problems in protracted intercommunal conflicts because it may exacerbate rather than ameliorate tension. It is important to be aware of the consequences of external aid on the dynamic nature of ethnic conflicts in order to avoid escalating conflict and doing harm through otherwise good intentions (ibid., 91). Instead, one must use a more organic approach. Peace building involves attempts to change negative attitudes by enhancing mutual understanding and respect (Love 1995) and involves socioeconomic development and reconstruction, restoring, rebuilding, and reconstructing new relationships (Curle 1990; Jeong 1995; Lederach 1997, 1999a, 1999b). Working on common economic problems promotes the contact necessary to challenge unrealistic perceptions of the other that go unchallenged on a daily basis in NI (Wright 1987). The aim of reconciliation is to sustain peace at both the micro- and macrolevels. Without contact and reconciliation, there can be no sustainable peace built within NI (Love 1995).

Within protracted ethnic conflict situations, funding agencies must think of the short versus long-term implications of their intervention actions. Funders must allow local grassroots groups to commission them to assist them through the process of grant applications. Moreover, funding agencies must develop clear funding categories that connect directly to the constructive transformation of the conflict (Lederach 1997, 91). For example, a major criticism of the EU Peace I Fund to NI suggests that it was passed and implemented too quickly, resulting in a lack of focus, little clarity of objectives, and problems with the indicators used to evaluate the program (Harvey 1997, 2003).

Moreover, the constructive conflict and peace-building approach emphasizes the shared responsibility of funding agencies and local communities in using economic resources for peace building (Lederach 1997). Local community groups must protect their own needs and not compromise or repackage their objectives to meet the criteria of the funding agencies (Byrne and Irwin 2000, 2001). In addition, citizens within NI need to transform their consciousness to clear their minds of illusions, change their hearts, and "imagine a new society" (Boulding

1990). As Freire acknowledges, a deepened awareness of one's situation allows people to fully comprehend that (oppressed) situation as being a reality open to transformation (1999, 6).

In contrast, economic development may have very little impact on the relationship between communities locked in protracted ethnopolitical conflicts because of the hidden violence deeply embedded in the societal structure (Pearson 2001). Ethnic rivalry and competition is used in NI as a political mechanism in the distribution of economic resources (Agnew 1989; Harris 1972). In the past, there was little opportunity for Catholics while Protestants enjoyed all of the economic privileges of a Populist regime in Belfast (Bew et al. 1979, 1995; Farrell 1980).

Up until the paramilitary cease-fires and the Mitchell–de Chaliand peace negotiations, the conflict was perceived as a way of life as people experienced the conflict firsthand on a daily basis. An apathetic world-view and an acceptable level of violence ensured that a sense of death, destruction, and hopelessness permeated the minds of most people living in NI (Byrne 1997). These feelings of death and the fear of violence may have changed in the wake of the current peace-building process.

Following is a discussion of what the respondents found salient in their perceptions of how external economic assistance may be building cross-community ties, reconciliation, and intracommunal work. It focuses on the respondents' interpretations of the impact of external economic assistance in building a peaceful and just society in NI.

Reconciliation and Peace Building

A widely held image of both IFI and EU Peace I funding held by respondents was that while economic assistance can serve to build peace, it must be linked to a political settlement that provides for equality in political, social, and cultural areas in order to transform conflict effectively within the NI context. In particular, community activists were critical that economic development was being substituted for real political change and that many of these new economic projects might provide unskilled labor opportunities with little prospect for long-term sustainability, an outcome likely to reinforce negative attitudes to political authorities and cynicism regarding the peace process.

A civil servant in Dublin suggests that businesspeople on both sides of the border have a powerful incentive to work together to access IFI and EU Peace I funding:

I think that Northern businesspeople and Southern businesspeople on some of our sector projects are coming together, and they could not care less what the bottom fix is. Therefore, it is bringing them together more so than any other reason because there is a sensitive issue there for the two sides to sit down together and there are some collaborative projects.

He adds:

We are trying to create better economic conditions so that there is less emphasis on the violence of the process. It will not make the political settlement happen, but it will mean that people on the ground are less attracted by the extreme philosophy that is on any side. So you are promoting a more fertile ground for acceptance of any settlement, promoting some kind of local stability, which people will be eager to accept a political stability that cuts across all of Northern Ireland.

In addition, another Dublin civil servant believed that the EU Peace I funding program is successful. This is what he had to say on the issue:

I think the Peace and Reconciliation Program played a great and good role at helping to maintain linkages between both communities. You could do a statistical analysis and say that the program failed. The Rowntree Report said that the peace program was meant to promote peace and undermined the peace process. The peace process broke down, the ceasefire broke down, therefore, the program failed. That's a very simplistic and unfair point of view. But it was very successful, I would say, in very difficult circumstances, but the success was one of maintaining a very modest development rather than a great success.

Similarly, a Peace I development officer in Co. Cavan is of the opinion that economic development has assisted the peace process by getting people actively involved:

The building up of an economic project that even creates small businesses rather than leaving people to float at the margin, to become marginalized and then turn away or get into antisocial activities if you like is critical. As the old saying goes, "the devil finds work for idle hands." So if you can create activity to get people working, doing something positive for the community, you can keep them on the straight and narrow if you like.

In addition, a community group leader in Co. Monaghan maintains that people with employment and a hopeful future are less likely to be involved with paramilitary organizations. He also believes that economic assistance is making a peaceful solution to the conflict possible:

One of the philosophies we have is that you never see a bank manager running out with a submachine gun. Or you do not see anyone in a reasonably paid job saying, "I am going to blow up a building tonight." The person with the full belly is less tempted to get into trouble. And I know in my heart and soul that you are never going to bring everyone up to a standard where everything is all equal.

He adds:

I think we have to put all that behind us and start from an even keel and recognize the wrongs that were done, and what is done is done and can't be really overturned. We have to recognize the hurt and the pain and everything that people have felt. You can't live in the past. You have to look forward to a new future. You know, I think that people tend some-times not to want to look at the history, and look at it logically and then say, "Well, that was then and it was a pity and it is different now." I think if we were all a wee bit more open and just give the other person the chance to say their piece and give them the chance to be wrong, I think that we might be right. I think that we are making giant steps unnoticed to our-selves. . . . I think that historical injustices done by both sides should be openly discussed and mourned or apologized for to close the book once and for all, unless you are a historian and you just take pleasure in read-ing history. History is a very dangerous thing if it is not broad enough; if it is given from one point of view. It is actually more dangerous than the bomb and the bullet, because it can indoctrinate young people, and this is what has tended to happen.

Another community group leader in Co. Cavan makes the point that contact along the border is happening between the Unionist and Nation-alist communities. However, he suggests that hard-core paramilitary ele-ments who do not favor intercommunal contact will not be co-opted into the peace process by the external funding agencies:

The more people see opportunities, the more they forget about the petty historical thing going back to their grandfather or their whatever, and the more on the one side they forget about King Billy of the Boyne, and the more on the other side they forget about 1916 and British oppression and whatever, and they get on with their life. The more good sustain-able employment you have, the more wealth creation you have, the more people look forward and the less they look backward. Most important of all, it gets a lot of people out of what I call the stagnant net and in the larger areas of population of NI, particularly Belfast. Whatever, you will find that people who for example, on either side who are most mercenary and most entrenched in their ideas and will not change, and will not move, ironically are those who are most downtrodden, most economically deprived, and most disadvantaged, and would appear to be, whether it is consciously or subconsciously, those people unknown to themselves who are being totally exploited. They have nothing to look forward to. An idle mind is the devil's disciple. . . . You will find that the most open people, the most confident people, and the most successful people, and I mean successful in the broad sense, not just in terms of how wealthy they are, how successful they are in terms of how content they are and how happy they are with their own lot, and that can range, you know. There is a big span there. You find that most of those people, they have a big interest in something or other. They are very happy in it and they look forward to it. But if you have nothing to look forward to, you are in my humble opinion in a limbo state, a permanent state of limbo. You have a stagnant mentality and every other way, and there are so many barriers on all sides of you preventing you to look at even the medium-size picture, not alone the big picture. . . . So suddenly in a very small period of time in economic cycle terms from 1970 to 1997, you now have a situation where, instead of being a peasant downtrodden society, you now have us being one of the leading countries in the world. A fairly small country, 3.5 million people in the Republic, a small island. Suddenly now they are talking about the Celtic Tiger in international terms, and that is good. Like any country it has problems, but nothing like the past . . . Bring more people together and everyone gives their views on all those things. And then you get to know the difference and the way things are working on both sides. There are hard core on both sides. No matter what peace and reconciliation you put in or money you put in, it's not going to work. It is not a question of money at all. I would think at our level here. Yes there is a couple of hard core. It may not be massive. There is a spin-off and there is movement I would say. But I mean you cannot control half a dozen.

Moreover, a community group leader in the Protestant Fountain enclave in Derry strongly supports the fact that economic aid can provide employment and build the self-esteem of the people in local communities. However, he warns that economic development projects should not create unskilled jobs for the poor because it will forever damage their self-esteem and self-efficacy.

Of course economic development is really important because it would give the young people here hope of getting a job and being able to stay in the Fountain. But if all this Peace money merely creates another series of short-term, unskilled jobs that will disappear when the funding dries up, then this community will not see much in the way of a peace dividend either in terms of their own economic situation or for Protestants in general, and their perception of the peace process as a sham will be affirmed, and a dangerous disenchantment with the whole peace process would likely emerge.

An important image held by the respondents was that while economic assistance is a critical element to build the peace dividend, it has to be linked to a political settlement that provides for socioeconomic, cultural, and political equality for all citizens to build a long-term peace settlement.

A senior civil servant in Dublin points out that the NI conflict is tied to a wider structural question, the political role of both governments. Also, implicit in his interview is the perception that the Intermediary Funding Bodies, by reaching down into the communities, have played a critical role in promoting peace and reconciliation.

> The cross-border sub-program and the peace program have been success-ful and have done it. And has done it not just at the grassroots level. It has done it at a public level as well as at a local level. So that's been a great success story of the peace program, one of the great success stories, so that's being positive. I think IFI and the EU Peace and Reconciliation Program has been more successful at reaching the marginalized within the two communities in the North than it has been in generating a great deal of new cross-community contact. But it certainly has generated a degree of new cross-community contact and has maintained what contacts were there very well. At a time, which is probably the time when the two communities in NI in the last two years were polarizing at a more rapid pace than ever before in the previous twenty-five years, following Drumcree. The peace program brought people together across the community divide.

A community leader from Derry believes that the conflict is not about changing perceptions, because external funding is not addressing real socioeconomic and power issues within society:

> Well, the basis of everything we do is that all cross-community and peace and reconciliation work should be beginning from the problem and acknowledging the problem and actually talking about it and not trying to cloak it all the time with very wavy words like perception, the percep-tion that each community has of the other. When I was doing my degree in peace studies, we did this part of the Quaker peace education project. It was a series of workshops that we did with them and a lot of it was about perceptions. "What are your perceptions now?" He was going to role-play an RUC man. "What is your perception now?" I said, "Wait a minute. A lot of this is not perceptions, it is reality. It is what people actually do face on the ground. It is not a perception." That is trying to bring everything into some very nebulous psychological word. People have got the wrong idea in their heads, and if they would only change those ideas, we would be all right. There are actually real issues involved here. There are also issues of power and money, and employment and power within the soci-ety. I just think that external funding should actually be concentrating on inequality within the society.

Another community leader in Derry suggests that external funding has raised people's expectations. He is concerned that when the external assistance ends, the people will become angry and despondent. He believes that the political conflict must be addressed before real reconciliation can take place within and between both communities. The development of economic projects, he argues, will impact confidence within each community in its own ability to concentrate its energy in "single-identity" projects before it is empowered to reach across the sectarian divide to the other community:

> I have to say it has made a difference. It has made a difference of—there are two sides to this—giving us resources that we did not have. We have people working who would not be working without this money. There is a potential that some of the projects will have long-term benefits. The problem, I think, is that it has raised expectations, and those expectations are not being met. In the longer term, it could create a real serious anticlimax, where people's jobs finally run out. The project has not had sufficient time to develop to the level it should have. . . . The terms and conditions of Peace and Reconciliation allows people to develop their own projects, which allows them to understand, which gives them a job, is a step toward peace. Reconciliation, I think, is a broader issue. I think that reconciliation can only go to a certain level and the broader issues are not involved.

In contrast, an IFI consultant for the border counties believes that the IFI has given a psychological boost to border communities by bringing investment to deprived areas, empowering and giving responsibility to local communities to come together to rebuild the community's socioeconomic infrastructure.

> IFI funding has helped the level of optimism. There has been a huge amount of community empowerment that has taken place as a result of the funds' activities, which I think has been very positive and has brought in a new confidence to people in the area. It has helped to defuse a lot of suspicions of the cross-border activities, like say, for example, the Wider Horizons program, which has brought together particularly youth groups from the two communities, North and South. That has done an awful lot to dispel the myths that have surrounded sectarianism, and you would often come across practical examples of that. There is a story from Derry and the situation of the marching season last year where a group of kids had been involved in Wider Horizons and knew their neighbors from across the river who they were about to throw stones [at] but held off. There was a couple of very tense situations defused there by the fact that these people had spent time together, and I think it is interesting to say that just in the last few days that we have seen an attitude of compromise emerging from the Nationalist community in Derry in relation to the marches. I think that a lot of that is stimulated and is helped and reinforced by

both funds. I am not saying that it has been done by the IFI investment or completely precipitated by that investment, but it has certainly been reinforced by projects like Wider Horizons, which has touched on large numbers of people, tens of thousands of people, who have undergone the Wider Horizons experience.

In contrast, an EU Peace I community development officer in Co. Cavan believes that economic aid has not fostered reconciliation and peace because the conflict is embedded in people's cognate schemata from a very early age. Thus, he suggests that only nonpolitical, nonthreatening issues are discussed in cross-community encounters. He expresses reticence about people's desire to hold political or religious conversation in the public forum. Instead, he suggests that it is more appropriate to focus cross-community discussions on superordinate goals:

> The people in the North are lovely people, I find them very nice. But there is some kind of thing. It is hard to characterize what it is, but it is there, and I have a feeling that they seem to run with it. Over the years I have paid compliments to them, and everything is okay as long as it is down to the conversation, and it does not drift into religion or politics. Now it is the same in meeting with these fellows on the community committees. Politics or religion is rarely discussed. We discuss the achievement and we discuss the things that are common to all of us, but the political aspect does not come into it.

Moreover, a community group leader in Derry questions the sincerity of people who promote peace at any cost. He is suspicious of people who act in this way. Instead, he suggests that both communities should strive for economic growth that spills over into peace. One method of accomplishing this obligation, he argues, is by empowering young people to focus on superordinate goals. For example, he has taken Unionist and Nationalist youth to work together on a building project in South Africa so that they could learn a wide range of social, political, and problem-solving skills. Moreover, he contends that the people of NI have twenty years to reconcile their bigotry and to build a culture of peace or face a Bosnia or Rwanda type of political chaos:

> I think that if economic development allowed people to come together and work together for a bigger objective than peace, it would be better. If you work together for peace sake, it is not as good as what we get for growth sake. So working together for peace sake, I think, is a very fragile thing. And I will not work just for the sake of peace. I just would not deal with that, and I have been confronted up in a major reconciliation center and I said that "I do not work for peace. I just work for growth." So, if you work for peace and no growth, then you can forget about it. If you

work for growth, the chances are that growth itself will lead to peace. So, economic development is absolutely essential if it allows the people to come together, such as we are trying to do when we take people, groups of Catholics and Protestants away to Africa to build houses for a black lady. . . . So, what I am saying is that economic development with the tag of money for reconciliation has not to be about peace. It has to be about working together to produce a better future. And unless we talk about peace, then there would be conflict, talk about the problems, get the hurt out, talk about it, and then let people own their bigotry. . . . But we have fifteen years, maybe twenty at the most, to come together. And I think that peace and reconciliation is absolutely essential, but how to go about it? It has to be real. It has to be real people dealing with real problems, problems that are bigger than themselves, preferably problems that they have reached to the sky in some way in order to achieve some greatness. The money is there but how the money has got to be used is vitally important.

In addition, a development officer with the EU Peace I Fund in Monaghan town adds that the IFI and the EU Peace and Reconciliation Program's focus is more on regional investment than on deep reconciliation as an integral part of the peace-building process:

If you look at EU programs in Bosnia and South Africa, there is a much more explicit peace-building element, and you have to admit that in this program there isn't that explicit peace-building element. There is cross-border reconciliation and there is the cross- community thing, but in terms of things that I would have liked to have seen and which the Combat Poverty Agency wanted to see in the program, it actually was in terms of civic education, in terms of explicit reconciliation-type element in everything. I think that the reconciliation was left out and I think that you could argue that. That bit's missing from the programs. And really the programs some would say is just another regional investment program without having any reconciliation imprint in every aspect of its being and that's one of the things that I'm worried about, and one of the things that the Rowntree Report points out. The EU Peace and Reconciliation package is a very conservative program compared to other EU programs, and as I say, there isn't this explicit peace-building thing built into it, which worries me.

Further, a community leader from Enniskillen, Co. Fermanagh, suggests that what is needed to change the nature of the conflict is not neutrality, but the development of trust between both communities. Here are his further remarks on this point of view:

I think that economic aid has played a role in cross-community development in that people have started to realize that if they can get together, very often I think it has encouraged people to start to communicate with other people within their community, and it is almost seen as a desirable thing to be doing. . . . Maybe I am being too critical. It probably challenged people to think about how it could impact on peace and reconciliation, and maybe in the longer term, it will do. But one of the things that I would be very, very careful about is of substituting social inclusion for peace and reconciliation. The other would be of trying to achieve do-gooders' admissions to building premises under the guise of neutral venues. If there ever was words in God's creation that gets my hackles up and anger up, is neutral venues. We are never going to get anywhere in this community until we start to embrace each other's tradition and get the courage to walk into somebody else's venue. Somebody reckoned that a neutral venue may be halfway. It won't be, and if you take a rural venue, for instance, or a sparse rural area which you are familiar with in this part of the world. In most instances there are already far too many venues in dilapidated state, falling apart, and all of a sudden there is funding made available for this flavor of the month concept of a neutral venue to the detriment of the local church hall, the sports hall, or the community hall. All of a sudden it is seen as the chic thing to do.

The problem is not a community problem or having a better understanding of the other. A community leader from Derry depicts political cynicism in his worldview. He thinks that the Peace and Reconciliation industry within NI has picked up on the British government's portrayal of the conflict as a problem between both communities:

Well, in very grassroots terms, the analysis of the conflict here, which comes from the Peace and Reconciliation or Community Relations industry, is that this is a community conflict. In other words, the basic problems that we face in this society are two communities that are in conflict with each other, and that is the basis of the problem—trying to break down barriers and create understanding and get people to work together and to go to school together and to live together and so on and so forth on the basis that if they understood each other better there would be less conflict. Now, we would argue that this analysis is shared very much by the British government, who wished to portray that analysis to the rest of the world because in doing so they escape their own involvement. An example I will give you. I had a conversation with somebody in England two nights ago who read our document on the Orange Order, who thought it was very good, but she also says, "You know, until the two communities really learn to tolerate each other, people should be able to march everywhere." I said, "I would like that as well, I think that would be an ideal solution. But what you are doing is you are pinning the whole problem on these two communities. You are forgetting the fact that the British government played a significant role:

(1) in denying one community the right to march because Catholics in Portadown have never been allowed into the center of town and that's a state decision ultimately, and (2) it is the British government who has forced the march through the Garvaghy Road for three years in a row."

According to another community group leader from Derry, the EU Peace I Program does not fund Irish-language groups, which are perceived by the funding personnel as Nationalist organizations. Here are his further remarks on this point of view:

So if the architects of some of these groups' intention was that they would be arbiters of Nationalist rights and Unionist rights, what you're landed up against is a crowd of safe characters, many of whom are from old, tiptoeing down the middle line of green pound, orange pound to try and adjust the failure. Now, I can understand why funders need to be assured of a safe pair of hands handling any money that was allocated, but giving it to the people who obviously know some aspects, but they haven't transformed society peaceably. For all the groups on the outside that are still trying to get in are excluded by these people because it's an old crowd network carving up a pie almost. I mean, they could be odd about it. Now, I'm attempting to criticize the fact that they do some good, but if this is specifically for peace, people are being asked to be patient, given hope they'll change, given hope that a few years down the line they're going to do excellently again. And the question of what has changed is coming to real life, which is not much will have changed.

Similarly, another prominent community group leader from Derry believes that Republicans were initially excluded from the funding process. He outlines why he believes that the layers of government bureaucracy safeguard the processing of economic resources to community groups. Here is his picturesque description of the civil service's role in the distribution of funds:

So the system is built in such a way that they try to safeguard themselves, that the money is not used for the wrong purposes and things like that, and that's why the Social Democratic and Labour Party made the cardinal sin in those early days when Sinn Féin was getting off the ground of saying to the government that these are revolutionaries and they shouldn't be getting money. I find that terribly wrong and no doubt of that in mind. The church also became involved in that one. The church became involved and the church was playing a big, big game in making sure that the money was pushed into areas where the SDLP were in power. I was very fortunate that I had friends in both camps, and maybe I was too strong for the SDLP to stand in my way because we were well established. We were well established before any of this money came in.

In a similar vein, another community group leader from Derry suggests that there is a lot of credibility built into which organization gets access to economic resources, and this is a problem for new groups who are starting out and who are applying for funding to the various agencies:

> There is a real lack of sustainability in all of the Peace and Reconciliation money. The majority of the money has actually gone from the employee over a period of three years to develop projects. Now once the funding runs out after a period of two or three years, there is no money available to actually keep people on as employees. So what happens to the projects that they have developed or started? I mean, there is obviously a stopping process there because how can you sustain the projects when you go through a length of period whenever there isn't the money to fund the employees. A lot of people said, "Right, we want to do community relation projects, but we want to employ someone specifically to take the lead role in it," which I think is fair enough. But the Community Relations Council had to say to a lot of organizations, "Look, beware this funding ends after a period of two years and you are unlikely to become core-funded from our organized core funding within the CRC, because we don't have that sort of money to allocate out." So the bottom line is, I think, there is a sustainability problem with some of the projects that have begun. I do know that there has been a major review of the Intermediary Funding Bodies, and they are talking about a second chance of the money coming through in September of this year (1997). Now if that comes through, I think there will be much more specific criteria for applications for that money. I actually think quite a larger proportion will go to the likes of the CRC to actually fund other organizations who are specifically dealing with reconciliation projects.

Their narratives illustrate an insight of occurrences in everyday life on both sides of the border. Some respondents hold an optimistic view, believing that a permanent cessation of political violence will empower the economic development process both within NI and along both sides of the border region. These respondents argue that economic assistance can reduce young people's support for political violence and create a political climate that promotes contact and prosperity to forge a peaceful NI society.

In addition, a community leader from Derry believes that the IFI and the EU Peace I Fund have played critical roles in building an economic infrastructure and in getting funds to the community groups on the ground. However, he is critical of the IFBs and the British governmental departments as not having absorbed the philosophical ethos of the EU Special Support Program because he perceives that former prime minister John Major's Conservative government was not an active supporter of the peace process:

I think that the IFI has done good work. The EU demonstrated consider-
able foresight in their decision to deliver on the Special Support Program
of Peace and Reconciliation with the inception of the IRA cessation of
violence in 1994. I think it demonstrated foresight and great courage, and
I think it is symptomatic of the progressive nature of mainland European
political discourse at social development and economic planning. It is
symptomatic of that. However, while that core philosophy underpins the
EU Special Support Program, and the ethos was there, there was a problem I believe, with the transferal of the ethos to the IFBs. Several of them
in my view did not have an appreciation of what exactly their work should
be seeking to achieve in political—with a small "p"—terms on the ground.
It has certainly been noticed by us that the British government departments and the Department of Finance and Personnel specifically have
utterly failed to absorb the ethos of the Special Support Program or to
demonstrate any appreciation for building a peace process. . . . It stands
to reason that the perspective did not trickle down into the media and the
civil service departments. And for that reason they were neither demon-
strating political commitment to the actual Special Support Program, the
European money, and they were not bringing to bear the flexibility and
communication and participation with this society to make sure that we
are not left out to derive from the Special Support Program. That is an
example of where we had a dichotomy between the ethos of the Special
Support Program and how it could help contribute significantly to work
on the ground. But it was strangled, emasculated in many senses by the
fact that the British government had not signed up with the political will
to make the process work at that stage.

In contrast, a community leader from Derry outlines how Scandinavian countries have developed socioeconomic development models that
effectively transformed their local economies. He elaborates that NI
needs to learn from and emulate these types of socioeconomic models
that involve grassroots organizations within both communities to nurture local indigenous economies:

I would argue that a number of things should happen if we were to cement
the macrolevel of the peace process. I think you would have to cement
that macrolevel. I think we also have to be building from the bottom up.
So, therefore, I think we need to have an investment in capacity building
of grassroots organizations. . . . The absolutely only way I can see you
doing that is to have a structure that builds up the social and economic
elements together. And I am saying the only way I can see that is the
social economy. We have to tackle the big issue of long-term unemployment. And we have to tackle this issue of growing youth unemployment
and disenfranchised young people. I still think that the only way you can
do that within those localities is through an enabled theme to work for
social economic development, which is a realistic approach to the local

environment. Now I have not got any sort of meat on the bone there, but I think it is possible. All I'm saying is if I look at other regions where they have been experimenting and possibly involved in socioeconomic development, a lot longer than we have, if you go to some of the Scandinavian countries, there are models there to be learned.

Moreover, a community leader from Derry highlights a concern vis-à-vis the British government's behavior in the distribution of the EU Peace I Fund within NI. He elaborates on public expenditure cuts and the quality of employment emerging out of the peace package. In addition, he fears that if the peace and reconciliation process fails, then the voluntary community sector will be scapegoated and blamed for its lack of success:

> I think as well, there is a lot of cynicism about how the last government kind of managed the NI economy. Like even the way they had major public expenditure cuts in areas that the peace package was funding. It was a separate peace package, not additional. . . . I have seen projects set up by local people creating jobs, and creating employment opportunities within that community for themselves, and that they don't get the support from the training and agencies—the government employment body—because they are saying, "We are not accrediting you as an employment training project, because you don't fit within our guidelines." And yet this is a training site. They are up against a difficult situation.

He adds:

> The district partnerships are currently being seen as a good form of local democracy, because they need to bring all the sides together and all the political parties together in a way that never happened before. I think what is left is social inclusion. Certainly social inclusion, peace and reconciliation is not taking place if there is no social inclusion, and if social inclusion did not work, what was the main bedrock of social inclusion and community development?

Some of our respondents highlight the centrality of transferring power from government bureaucracy to the grassroots level. They illustrate the importance of decision making and power in the distribution and control of funds. It would appear that the experience of these groups is a key determinant in their attitudes toward the funding process. Some are of the opinion that both IFI and EU Peace I funding has assisted in restoring pride to local communities, while others argue that single-identity politico-economic and psychological needs must be worked on within each community before it can reach across the sectarian divide to work with members of the other community. As a community leader from Derry explains:

It's the same again as those cross-community things, where Catholic Christians go into Protestant Christian churches, and they shake hands and they all come out and say, "It was wonderful. I met a real Protestant," or "I actually touched a Catholic." These aren't the people who were waging the war. We know that they are pacifist, we know they are stable. I'm not saying that you brave the areas where violence is coming from. Violence is a symptom of pain and suffering, and that's what this city's addressing.

CROSS-COMMUNITY TIES

In this section we explore the images of respondents regarding the question of whether IFI and EU Peace I funding has promoted cross-community ties, which both funding agencies view as important to the building of a sustainable peace within NI. Most suggest that both communities must empower themselves before they are secure enough to work on cross-community development projects. The respondents do suggest, however, that cross-community projects that require groups to work together to access funding have begun to dispel some fear felt by community members in working with those from other communities.

The following respondents are of the opinion that funds from the IFI and EU Peace I may not be promoting cross-community contact, despite the optimism of the donors and, in some respects, escalating competition for funding between the communities.

A community group leader in Co. Fermanagh is of the opinion that economic aid has played a significant role in the institutionalization of a sustainable peace process in NI. Yet he questions if economic assistance can transform relationships between both communities. He argues that what is needed to transform the conflict is contact and the development of trust between both communities.

I think that it has played a role in cross-community development in that people have started to realize that they can get together. Very often I think it has encouraged people to start to communicate with other people within their community, and it is almost seen as a desirable thing to be doing. . . . Maybe I am being too critical. It probably challenged people to think about how it could impact on peace and reconciliation, and maybe in the longer term it will do. But one of the things that I would be very, very careful about is of substituting social inclusion for peace and reconciliation. . . . I do not think that it is by sanitizing our traditions that we are going to solve our problems. And I am very concerned that the integrated schools are doing this. It is a nice anodyne sanitized version of Ireland. Again the middle-class solution coming into it of what society should be like. And we all in this country inherit a wealth of culture going back over to different flash points, but we do not throw the baby out with the bathwater. We do not put our cultures into cold storage. Because you saw what happened in Bosnia when it went into cold storage. When it thawed, by God, it erupted. We need to start to understand and endure the pain of trying to understand each other's culture, and not even accepting each other's culture. We need to try to understand where the other side is coming from, and try to learn that we have to respect where they are coming from, whether we like it or whether we do not. It's all about looking at the way. And this is the one danger that I keep coming back to; that is the danger of Peace and Reconciliation and IFI money being used for that particular purpose.

A community group leader in Derry is even more adamant that the funding has not encouraged both communities to work together to create change. He suggests cross-community work was there long before the funding, and that these groups focused on sharing skills and knowledge, not in reconciling differences. Further, he makes the point that these groups are from the working-class grassroots community and do not have the middle-class and professional status and appearance desired by the funding agencies:

The money has copper-fastened a lot of the work that has been going on anyway. Whether the money is going to help initiate new projects, you know, new cross-community projects for the sake of making change rather than for the sake of using money, I think is something that would need to be looked at. The money has not made it happen. It has been happening. It just made it better. And there are areas where contact across the community divide is as difficult now as it ever was. But I can think of areas around NI where it would be seen as extremely polarized. . . . I mean the biggest changes, some of the most violent methods of reducing violence across the community divide, would be happening with small groups who have not got a visible profession. I mean, that is important. People are where they come from. You know they have not lost that. And they have not felt the need to professionalize the whole approach so that they can get it over to them.

Another community group leader in Derry also argues that economic self-interest to cooperate across the ethnoreligious divide is not a sufficient reason for the Unionist and Nationalist communities to work together. Instead, he points out that a moral imperative is needed if both communities are to live in some kind of harmony together:

There will be answers, which have a consistency and continuity beyond two or three years and will not be short-term answers. And they will not simply be to do with that. We learn to live together because of economic self-interest. Which it might be. It probably is. But that is not sufficient. We learn to live together because of some moral imperative. We learn to live together because it is in our own best interest and we have come to that conclusion. And out of that, you can develop all sorts of philosophies and economics and whatever.

A community leader from Clones, Co. Monaghan, suggests that Protestants and Catholics are getting together despite intimidation from hardline members of their communities. He also explains how the Thatcher government framed the unemployed as lazy rather than deal with the underlying structural inequalities within NI:

Peace and reconciliation. Here is Protestants and Catholics getting together to do something. Again, so much of it works by strength, by creeping up on people and getting them to do things and persuading them that way rather than getting to the pulpit and preaching to them, and this has happened. We were up in Tyrone and a local group, Protestants in the group, great and they could work away grand, cross-community group. But then something happened and publicity in the papers and so on and that they dropped out because with fears of intimidation that the extreme side of the things put forth its ugly head. But even during the peace we had here, I noticed it was a problem up here, for example, because it was tried to be got for plays by basically a Catholic group, and they said it was not available with insurance and all that kind of thing. We knew in various ways that there was intimidation. But during the peace it has changed, but building up the economy and giving jobs to people doing away with the dereliction. The dereliction alone was labeling the place that it was falling apart. It was ugly, and you had no pleasure walking up the street. All these things can have an effect on people's attitude and they become aggressive. . . . I know we have a problem as far as the boundary line is concerned. Ms. X crosses it every morning on her way to work. But we would like to think that it doesn't exist. It's psychological, the line is psychological, and that we can sell the area and that somebody tries to find the line, and if they can't find it then, that is not there. That is the picture that we would like to present.

These colorful individual narratives presented by these respondents illustrate the apparent difficulty in ending the political violence. Also, these respondents highlight the intractability of the conflict that makes any future resolution difficult. In these descriptions note also that economic development has given a psychological boost to the empowerment of community groups. The viewpoints of some of the community group leaders also indicate that a political solution is necessary to transform the conflict. These respondents are aware that the all-party political process will be significant in any movement toward a just and lasting peace in NI. They also advocate for clear measures of accountability on the part of both the funding bodies as well as those community groups receiving economic assistance.

Intracommunal Single-Identity Projects

In this section respondents' views about whether IFI and EU Peace I aid has fostered cross-community ties are examined. Both funding agencies view this as being important in transforming the conflict and building peace in NI. Most suggest that despite the optimism of the donor agencies, the funding may not be having the desired effects.

According to an EU Peace I development officer in Co. Tyrone, a startling 3 percent of the funding is going to cross-community reconciliation projects. Instead, he believes that the bulk of the money is going to single-identity projects that promote a bottom-up economic development approach within each community:

> I will never suggest it shouldn't be spent. I think it is good money, and I think by and large those projects are good projects. And I don't have a problem with it and it is a bottom-up focus and disadvantaged-oriented. So once again I don't have a problem with that either. But it is just the fact that I don't think there is no real push for reconciliation.

In addition, a Nationalist community leader from Derry suggests that economic assistance is shaping a new society by targeting economic inequality and neglect. However, he elaborates that the focus of the economic restructuring must be on the single identity of each community because of the "siege mentality" within the Unionist community. He believes that both the Nationalist and Unionist communities must develop their own economic needs before they can begin to work together across the sectarian divide:

> Yes, economic development is an essential ingredient of any peace and reconciliation process. When societies have been at war and they need to be reconstructed—not just in terms of the morale and the social fabric of societies—and in societies such as this, which were catapulted into a conflict from a structure of profound neglect and inequality, there is a massive economic reconstruction which has to take place, and that has to take place on a very targeted basis. Areas that have been at the cold face of conflict are invariably areas which exhibit the highest incidence of inequality, unemployment, poor health, and low education, such as this area. And in turn there must be a commensurate investment of resources to those societies.

He adds:

I think the baseline for moving to a point where there can be a cross-community-led economic development is that individual communities, on a single-identity basis, need to be given the facilities and support and investment to be vitalized themselves on their own terms, and from a position of revitalization on the basis of equality rather than on the basis of suspicion.

In contrast, another community leader from Derry believes that both the IFI and the EU Peace I funds are being inclusive and are attempting to introduce participatory democracy at the grassroots level. For example, he is of the opinion that the partnership boards are encouraging people from both sides of the conflict to work together to allocate resources to the overall community:

The obvious one that springs to mind is that Europe is trying very hard to export its kind of pillars of openness, transparency, accountability, exclusivity, and participatory democracy. All of these are happening, you know, Europe is trying very hard for that. Europe has become graduated with giving a lot of money to IFBs which come from the voluntary sector and by that I'm talking about the NI Voluntary Trust [NIVT] especially. . . . But there is an alternative logo of sectarian politics that people can become part of a partnership board which is cross-sectional and representative, and that they have power to hand out money. And that they have to work together and that they are looking at issues. Whereas before they wouldn't have looked at cross-community issues because they all come from single-identity backgrounds. All that sort of stuff. That money from Europe is coming with a message. It's coming with a process. It's coming with a long-term commitment.

Moreover, a community leader from Derry strongly believes that reconciliation must not be forced on communities, as they need to be ready to work for it. He claims that peace and reconciliation is not happening through the peace process because only the people who are interested in peace are building ties across the community divide. Each community needs to develop its own identity before it can embrace and begin to work bilaterally with the other community. Economics on its own will not build a real peace:

First of all, peace and reconciliation, sometimes they are terms that are not well enough defined. I actually think sometimes that the reconciliation work that goes on here is almost a lie because of the whole nature of the situation. People are certainly part of what is happening now and will transform that. And there is no doubt sometime in the future, there will be that sort of creativity, as barriers break down, then people will want to mix. And then you will have that true form of reconciliation work.

And they are bringing people together, maybe Protestant and Catholic or whatever, but they are bringing them together in situations where they would come together anyway. It is hard to get examples of it, but people can apply to the CRC for money if they have a project and if it is a joint project. An example of it would be, we could have a debate tonight, and say we are going to look at the effect of imprisonment on both Loyalists and Republicans and invite some Loyalists down and he talks and you get a grant for him, and you can let on that that is a part of some sort of reconciliation process. But you know in your heart of hearts it is not . . . whereas the experience of Republicans and Loyalists may be similar as they get out [of prison], the way it is catered for can be very different in their own distinct areas. . . . They are bringing people together who are together anyway, and they are not making any great impact. Whereas I think if you start to create people's own identity, they become strong in their own identity, and when it comes to making the transformation they are no longer feared to say, "Right, if I have to go in there tonight and address Loyalists, they are not going to do it." Whereas at the minute, it is going to drop somebody in and say, "Here is the expert on it." That is where I see it now in terms of economic assistance. Yes it can help, but economic assistance is not the answer to establishing peace nor is it the answer to establishing reconciliation, and that is the other danger of this idea [of] funding. We will throw money at things, and that is not going to work on its own. Certainly, at all levels, politics has to be sorted out. The politics of this society has to be transformed and then underneath you can start building up all the layers.

Another community leader in Derry suggests that people who work in other community neighborhoods can be shot by paramilitaries. Individuals can also add their name to a project so that the other community can get their grant, but it's not being honest to cross-community reconciliation. He also thinks that the IFI wants visual projects:

There are few Protestants living in Rosemount. Now there are some, and we do have involvement of Protestants. If I was to say, for example, I am going to set up a community-based training information technology project and the funders come back and say, "We want cross-community involvement in the management of the project." What am I supposed to do? Go up to Irish Street and drag people from there and ask them to come and sit on a management committee? This is not realistic. We can set the aims of the project to be cross-community, we can build it as best as possible, and we can include cross-community work within it. I mean one of the things in one of the projects was to develop cultural awareness, and they said, "Will this include Protestant culture?" And we said, "We can try to understand it, but I can't involve Protestants unless they want to be involved in it," and secondly, for community groups in our community to be able to sit in a room even and talk to somebody from a different

community about their culture. You have got to understand your own culture first, and I believe that even understanding your own culture is a step
forward toward understanding others. Now you have a crowd coming
back saying, "This is not a cross-community project, therefore, you won't
get funding," and we say, "What will make it cross-community?" And they
say, for example, "Your usual group will be mixed Catholic and Protestant?" And I say, "If I lived on the Malone Road, I could probably achieve
that, but unfortunately, I don't. Now you tell me, if you can get Protestants
to come from Irish Street into the Bogside or the enrollment area or if it's
safe for our kids to go across to Irish Street . . . if you can guarantee that,
then we will do it." For example, I have one of our projects funded under
the Maiden City Welfare Rights, and it is funded to develop community
training in the Waterside Co-op, in Irish Street, and in New Buildings,
what would be perceived as Protestant areas. Right over the door was a
big sign saying, "Anyone who fraternizes with Taigs [Catholics] will be
shot!" The group who invited him over said to him, "Look Mickey, we
really appreciate what you are trying to do, but this is dangerous." What
do you say to that? It is part of our project. You have to go over, it is part
of our project. There is limits to what anybody can do. "Hands Across the
Community" is all very well, but I can't put my hand on their shirt, and
neither do I expect Protestants from the Fountain area to feel comfortable
coming down the Bog. I mean, I might quite openly say to them, "Look,
you have no problem here," but I can fully understand if they say, "You
might say that, Mr. X, but I really don't feel comfortable and I am not
really sure what I am doing there." If they apply for a cross-community
grant, they can put my name down, they have done this before. X Center
was going to be part of this, but in reality, I am putting my name on their
piece of paper to get them their funding. The funders in many cases know
this, but it is all due to them to turn a blind eye. But in honesty, if you turn
to honesty, then you are told you are not cross-community.

Another community leader from Derry thinks that the money has not
helped communities to work together to make things better; cross-community work was always there. The focus on these groups is on sharing
skills and knowledge, not in reconciling differences. These groups are
from the community and do not have the professional status and appearance desired by the funding agencies:

How people within both communities are making stuff happen? In
communities, they are still seen as two completely separate entities. But
individuals within those communities are involved in projects that are
making things happen that are crossing that divide—some of the things
in North Belfast probably, an area that has seen the bulk of sectarian
Troubles in Belfast. I know people who are from, you know, politically
poles apart in both Protestant and Catholic communities, you know, who
are working to defuse tensions. They wouldn't say they are promoting

peace and reconciliation. This is one of the things I think they wouldn't say obviously. They are shown how communities can work together to make things better. I mean, if that's promoting peace and reconciliation then that is fine. But I think with a number of people that would be the impression I would get would be that they would say, "No, this is not a reconciliation project." This is about sharing our skills, our experience, our plus and minuses with another community and allowing them to share their pluses so that we can find, you know, things that are common ground, things that we can change. The interesting thing is that a lot of the groups that are involved in that type of work wouldn't have the professional sort of image that the whole fault in criteria seems to see we need to have.

Another community group leader from Derry is of the opinion that economic self-interest and cooperation alone are not sufficient reasons for the Unionist and Nationalist communities to work together. Instead, a moral imperative should ensure that it is within both communities' interests to live in some kind of harmony together:

And would you turn to a university department and say, "Change the world. You are going to be getting the money for three years, and you haven't changed the world?" So, there needs to be loads of resources put into this work, but this is the real work that people on this island have been called upon to do. So that it is a great gift. It is a great opportunity that we will have for ourselves and for the rest of the world. And we are called upon to do it and we can all do it together. These are the questions facing civilization at the end of the twentieth century. These are the questions for the millennium and they are very basic and very raw and very brutal and barbarous. How can we learn to live together? With all of the sophisticated techniques and so on and technical wizardry, how can we learn to live together? It is as basic as caveman stuff. But there might be answers.

In addition, a Nationalist community group leader from Derry adds that the communities need constructive conflict to assist in creating constructive social change in NI's society. He suggests that people have to realize that sectarianism was imported from outside by the British monarchy and that both communities are not to blame for the continuation of the conflict. Bringing the people together right now in the hope that they will live together is not realistic when suspicion and distrust permeates the relationship:

Don't get me wrong, I welcome every single penny that we get from America, from the EU, or from anywhere else. Even if it's not going to where I think it should be going, it is not going to a loss. It is still going somewhere. At the end of the day it is not our fault that this situation exists. People keep looking at us and say, "Why can't they live together?" Why the f——k did they set it up in the first place and then ask us to resolve it? I didn't set up a sectarian system. I am not sectarian. I can be anti–Orange Order, but it doesn't make me sectarian. I believe the Orange Order to be a sectarian organization and to be anti–Orange Order is to be antisectarian, and if somebody says to me, "Can you appreciate Protestant culture?" I say, "Yeah, I can appreciate what Martin Luther said, I can appreciate a lot of Protestant culture, but what I don't appreciate is somebody who stomps around with f——n' orange badges on them telling me that I have to accept it, anymore than the black population of America would accept the Ku Klux Klan marching through their ghettos." I think it is time that people would stop this patronizing behavior, which comes to me and says, "Why can't you all live together if only we could appreciate each other's tradition?" I feel like turning round and saying, "Go away and f——k off. Give my head peace." I remember one of the peace things one time years ago. There was a crowd of women. Most of them were well-meaning people. Betty Williams and Mairead Corrigan were a different kettle of fish. They were in it for all they could get. But a lot of the women went across that bridge, and there was thousands of them, thousands saying "We want peace." I remember standing on the bridge, and [seeing] a person with a big banner and it had a big nation on it coming down on someone's head, and on the banner it says, "Go on away and give my head peace," and another one said "To promote the illusion of peace is but to prolong the war." I think there is a danger in this, that people are saying, "Peace means let's stop talking, let's stop annoying each other," and I don't believe that. I think that peace means the ability to be blaming each other without knocking the f——k out of one another. I think we should be able to argue without burning each other's flags. I can sit and I can tell the Orange Order and I can tell Protestants I do not like your Orange Order. I do not like the way they parade. I don't like what they do, and I have every right to say that. And because I say a thing like that doesn't make me sectarian anymore than the Fountain tomorrow turns around and says, "We do not want Sinn Féin [SF] marching through the Fountain." I wouldn't say that is sectarian. I would say that is the way they feel. That is their view, and we cannot impose our view on them. We can argue our view. We can try and convince them of our view. We can say, "Look, we really are not a threat to you." This is what all this is about, and we should really be the guard of this. But as long as those people say, "I don't want you in our area at the moment," you have to accept that.

Similarly, another Nationalist group leader from Derry believes that there is no neutrality within NI as a result of the structural violence of the state, which is imposed on both communities. The Protestant community is distrustful of Nationalists who advocate and work for peace. He believes that Unionists like to deal with "straight-up Taigs" because they know where they are coming from:

If you pin the problem on the individuals within a society, then basically, according to that wealth, you will create if you think positively. Therefore, all white people in the States think positively, so aren't they good, and black people think negatively, and aren't they unfortunate? I don't agree with that. I would go in for a much more structural criticism of this society and the one we live in, and what are the things that f—k people up and make them the way they are. I just don't buy into that stuff. I accept that the whole issue of self-esteem is a massive problem, but I think it raises people's self-esteem to stop an Orange march through Derry. If that's what people decide they should be doing and that is okay. There is also a pretense at neutrality, and that's one you have from me reiterating again and again. We are not neutral. We are firmly based within this community. Although we have got a very good track record in contacts that we would have with people within the Apprentice Boys and within the Unionist parties. I think they find it easier to accept us because they realize, "Well, that Taig [Catholic] here is straight-up, they tell you what they are." I think they have more of a problem with the Taigs who pretend not to be Taigs, and you take the example of St. Columbs Park House, wonderful facility. But St. Columbs Park House says, "This is a neutral venue." And on a recent document put out by the community, in North-West Community Network, one of St. Columb's Park House's leaders talks about the community blindness that he used to have when he worked in a community group up in the city center and they would organize meetings in the city center. They said, "We suffered from a type of community blindness because we did not realize that Protestants by and large wouldn't come to these meetings because they were not on the city side because they have all moved to the Waterside." So now his Center is in the heart of the Waterside, and he is saying, "We don't suffer from such community blindness anymore." Well for a start, the irony is his own Center was petrol bombed because he had an SF speaker at it even though the whole management committee is basically UDA and such, Glenn Barr and so on, and it's given as a neutral venue. But we don't see it as neutral. Now, if he would just say, "Well, we are not a neutral venue." But he says this is the big neutral venue, but it is not at all neutral. To get to St. Columbs Park House, you have to pass through a British army checkpoint on the road. For a lot of us, it is not exactly what we want to do. It is also many miles away, so for the vast majority of working-class people here, it is a taxi journey away. The place was opened by the [former] NI security minister John Wheeler. There was a big bouncy castle on the opening day for the kids to play on, and written across the top of the bouncy castle was "RUC Community Relations Unit." Now, as we said at the time, a lot of people in this community have gone through RUC bouncy castles. It wasn't air within them. It was walls, and they were being bounced off of them. That's not neutral for us. But it's this agenda that somehow the state is neutral. And then there is the two communities in conflict. That is absolute crap. Same agenda with Oakwood Integrated College, lovely place, great. But it's mostly the middle-class that are going to it, though not exclusively because there is a lot of people who don't want to send their kids to religious schools anymore. But I mean the agenda that there is in there. I mean several months ago the news came out. Well, it didn't come out publicly that we know of. We haven't publicized it, because the parents have asked us not to. They have tried to deal with it themselves within the school. It was when one of the parents went to pick up her child and saw an RUC man coming out and she said to her child, "What was he doing there?" She doesn't want to dump something on her child, and the child said, "He was in our class this morning under this series 'People Who Help Us.'" So it was an integrated class of Protestants and Catholics, and because it is integrated, they feel the need to go the whole way down the state line, and they had him in. Now not only that, but the guy brought a riot helmet and a riot shield with him and let the kids play with it. This was three months after three-hundred-odd people were injured in this city by plastic bullets last July. This was last autumn after incredibly bad riots where people were taken injured to the local hospital, were battened inside the casualty ward, and they had the cheek to invite the RUC into the school. Now we have got a problem with that. This is not cross-community to me. That is a state agenda, and I have got big problems with that. You will find that the funding that comes from the outside often looks like it's cross-community, bringing Catholics and Protestants together. Great! Get the money. Get a community center or a Peace and Reconciliation center in a Loyalist area trying to involve Loyalists who are so resistant to get involved.

These individual colorful descriptions presented by respondents illustrate the apparent difficulty in creating crosscutting ties across the ethnoreligious divide. These respondents are also aware of the significance of external economic assistance in impacting intracommunity economic growth.

DISCUSSION

This chapter has illustrated some issues that community groups, civil servants, and development officers find to be salient regarding the impact of economic assistance in building cross-community ties and reconciliation. In general, the respondents in this study had a variety of opinions about the role of economic aid in building a web of interdependent relations and a politically engaged community ready to collaborate and cooperate with each other to transform society. Some of the community leaders felt that "peace was a business," and that the aid was promoting single-identity rather than cross-community reconciliation projects. Civil servants and development officers felt that the economic assistance brought pride and responsibility to both communities, building their capacity, empowerment, self-esteem, and self-efficacy. Other respondents were of the opinion that economic aid is not a panacea to resolve the political conflict. Instead, structural inequalities and sectarianism exist within two deeply divided and entrenched communities. These respondents believed that each community needs to turn inward and build capacity before reaching outward to work for cross-community reconciliation.

Additionally, civil servants in Dublin illustrate that the funding process has promoted closer cooperation between civil servants both North and South of the border. Collaboration on a superordinate goal has spilled over into the political realm because both bureaucracies have to work closely together. Development officers within the agencies have also forged closer cooperative ties and serve local communities best because they understand their needs.

With regard to whether economic development facilitates, exacerbates, or is having no effect on the resolution of the NI conflict, some civil servants and community group activists believe that the peace process is tied to the wider political problem that is structural in nature. One possible reason that might suggest why there are similarities of opinion is that some of the participants believe that economic development alone will not bring a lasting peace to NI. Any legitimate and just resolution to the conflict will only emerge from a political process that includes both governments and the internal actors (McGarry and O'Leary 1995; O'Leary and McGarry 1993), a view held by a number of people within NI.

Similarly, some of the funding agency development officers and community group members in Derry and the border areas suggest that only a sliver of EU Peace I funding is going into cross-community projects. The majority of the money is funding single-identity projects to help rebuild the economic, moral, and self-esteem framework of each community. Part of the explanation for the focus on each community's independent economic development is that the Protestant community is suspicious of the funding agencies' perceived political agenda, and the Catholic community feels that it has to develop its own infrastructure before it can work with the Protestant community.

Thus, participants from across all four groups had different opinions about whether external economic aid was promoting peace and reconciliation. One set of opinions suggested that the money is getting into marginalized areas and is bringing pride and responsibility to local communities. The other set of opinions suggest that peace and reconciliation is not happening through the peace process, and that funding is not trickling down into marginalized and disadvantaged areas. "Peace has become a business," and when the money runs out, the voluntary groups who were working for peace and reconciliation before the onset of the funding process will be the only groups remaining who will continue to work in this area.

Others, within the less optimistic group, suggest that constructive conflict, not economic aid, is necessary to create social and structural change in the society. NI is a system of political problems. Therefore, we need to fractionate and interrelate the conflict resolution approaches to the conflict. For example, integrated education and grassroots economic development are an integral part of the peace-building process.

Most of the respondents in this study highlight the importance of IFI and EU Peace I funding by getting people involved to work together and promote cross-community development. Implicit in their stories is the view that the funding agencies have helped the peace process by providing jobs to keep young people out of paramilitary organizations. In contrast, some of the community group leaders in Derry suggest that economic self-interest and cooperation alone will not have Catholics and Protestants working together. Each community has to develop a single identity to harness its own energy, and both governments have to eliminate structural violence to transform the society and build a positive peace. These respondents suggest that there are other political structural issues as well as economic issues—alienation, political disenfranchisement, unemployment, poor quality of life, poverty, and hunger—occurring in society that do not augur well for the current peace process. These assumptions about structural violence are most probably the result of the fact that some of these respondents come from working-class backgrounds in Derry.

What does this all mean? There is a tension between cross-community ties and the goals of the funding agencies to create cross-community ties. A number of respondents are of the opinion that real reconciliation is not occurring. This is not surprising given that the conflict is deeply embedded in the psychology of both communities over a long period of time. Sensitive political issues are never discussed in public out of a fear of offending members of the other community. Other respondents suggest that efforts to create cross-community ties are shallow. Community leaders put their names down on grant applications so that the grant appears to be a cross-community application, even though that person is not really committed to the project. This form of cross-community cooperation is a good example of community leaders collaborating to "work the system" to gain access to the economic resources. Yet other respondents make the point that the economic assistance is promoting cross-community contact but extremists target those Protestants and Catholics who are working together, perhaps because they feel threatened that the partnerships will erode their power base in the grassroots community.

A large number of respondents in the urban areas are of the opinion that there cannot be mutual recognition and justice without empowerment. It is difficult to build awareness, reconciliation, and trust if there is power asymmetry in the society. An intracommunity or single-identity focus is empowering for Nationalists, who have suffered the brunt of impoverishment, and for Unionists to sustain their cultural identity in the wake of rapid political changes. Reenergizing the spirit within each community has brought pride back to local communities, kept young people out of the rival paramilitary organizations, and provided hope for a better future. Each community needs to build its own self-confidence before it feels comfortable reaching across the political divide to work with the other community.

This study leads one to the question, what do we mean by reconciliation and peace building, and what is the role of economic aid in this process? A psychocultural approach examines the process whereby identity is preventing people from addressing structural issues (Ross 1993). Psychocultural issues need to be addressed first to explore the needs of each group so that the structural issues can then be addressed. Do ethnic groups locked in conflict really want to transform their relationship? Are they really interdependent? Is it important to address identity issues before poverty issues or should a multitrack intervention process address subjective and objective issues simultaneously?

A number of respondents in this study suggest that the NI conflict is political and, therefore, demands a political solution. While external economic assistance is not a panacea, constructive conflict allows both communities to sustain their identities and sense of self. The 1998 GFA is a first tentative step on the road toward building a sustainable and lasting peace in NI. Unionist fears are allayed as NI remains part of the Union, and Nationalists perceive a real and tangible seismic shift in the commitment of the British government toward an eventual united Ireland. Moreover, the NI Assembly and power-sharing executives with devolved powers seek to build norms of cooperation among NI's political elites.

Consequently, economic assistance is tackling the economic issues and long-term inequalities that are an underlying cause of the NI conflict without necessarily changing dialogues between the Unionist and Nationalist communities. Dialogue groups, problem-solving workshops, and a constructive storytelling process can be used to address the psychocultural cause of the conflict (identity, fear, misperceptions) that prevent both communities from building a trusting relationship. These conflict resolution processes are critical tools for voluntary and conflict resolution organizations at the grassroots level in attempting to transform the relationship of both communities through a sustainable, imaginative, and creative peace-building process. This inductive approach facilitates a joint analysis of the deep-rooted fissures that divide both communities.

As Galtung (1996) suggests, structural violence is built into the structure of all cultural, socioeconomic, political, and legal institutions that deny self-worth, sociopolitical equality, and economic opportunity to the oppressed. Hidden violence or oppression in the structure eventually erodes human values and lives by forcibly stunting the development of any human being because of his/her ideology, religion, language, class, race, age, or gender (ibid.). Social justice embraces the idea of interdependent relationships based on the values of cooperation and Gandhian *satyagraha* (nonviolent pursuit of truth) and *ahimsa* (active love) to attain a desirable, sustainable, and just peace. Positive peace or justice necessitates, therefore, the creation of harmonious and nonexploitive socioeconomic and political structures (ibid.).

The findings are also reflective in some independent reviews of the programs. For example, the European Union Court of Auditors found that the IFI's evaluation of project applications and postgrant monitoring of projects did not "ensure sound financial management in all cases," whereas the EU's Special Peace and Reconciliation Program's selection and appraisal procedures "lacked common criteria," and an "effective methodology" for targeting community projects and social groups (EU Court of Auditors 2000, 11–12). Similarly, Harvey's report on the EU's Special Peace and Reconciliation Program highlighted the necessity of more rigor in program design to formulate appropriate indicators and measures to monitor the program's peace-building effectiveness (Harvey 1997, 84).

CONCLUSIONS

This chapter focused on the possible connections between the role of external economic assistance in generating sustainable economic development and nurturing cross-community ties and reconciliation to transform the conflict. Conflict resolution scholar-practitioners and policy makers need to consider the impact of external economic aid and its delivery. Moreover, they need to consider the impact of economic aid on postconflict local economies and how that intervention may promote sustainable economic development, conflict transformation, and a positive and just peace (Curle 1990; Jeong 2005; Lederach 1997). Underdeveloped local economies are not the main source of ethnoreligious conflict within NI; a complex intermeshing of structural, historical, ethnoreligious, and psychocultural factors are also salient (Byrne and Keashly 2000; Byrne and Carter 1996; Whyte 1990). However, external economic aid, properly administered, could contribute to the future deescalation of conflict within NI and other ethnopolitical conflicts such as in Bosnia, Cyprus, Darfur, East Timor, Iraq, and Rwanda because it builds up local economic infrastructures, and thus facilitates the use of other peace-building and transformative conflict resolution mechanisms to counterbalance psychocultural perceptions and feelings such as fear, hurt, and stereotyping among others.

This study of external economic aid to NI contributes to an understanding of the underlying structural and psychocultural factors at work in ethnopolitical conflicts so that peaceful change and coexistence can be built from the grass roots up (Byrne and Ayulo 1998; Byrne and Irvin 2000, 2001; Irvin and Byrne 2002). The respondents in this study suggest that to better understand the role of conflict resolution within ethnopolitical conflicts one must realize that local indigenous socioeconomic development must be encouraged if former enemies are to attempt to build a participatory democratic system.

Multitrack diplomacy (with an active citizens' track) can assist in also blurring the socioeconomic, political, and cultural boundaries that still form part of the bicommunal divide in NI. A national healing process (the Bloody Sunday Inquiry) similar to Archbishop Desmond Tutu's Truth and Reconciliation Commission in South Africa is needed in NI to deal with past injustices such as Bloody Sunday, the Shankill Butchers, Le Mons, and Remembrance Day in Enniskillen if the historical ghosts of the past are to be exorcised from NI's future, and the "transgenerational transmission of trauma" ended and not passed along to future generations (Volkan 1998). When people begin to work in an interdependent manner on economic issues, these economic norms may spill over into the political arena to forge a working peace system where conflict is both functional and institutionalized. This process of integration is similar to the economic and political development of the European Union.

7

Conclusions: Building Peace in Northern Ireland

INTRODUCTION

THIS BOOK ATTEMPTS TO BRING forth the perspectives of ordinary citizens, civil servants, and agency development officers who otherwise may not be heard. They speak about their political world, including socioeconomic development, politics, and the peace process. Their discussions are relevant to possible avenues for sustainable economic development and peace building in other ethnopolitical conflicts.

As ethnic cleansing became front-page news (Pearson 2001), in some respects the contemporary escalation of global ethnopolitical violence seemed to have confirmed "the clash of civilizations" or "the coming anarchy" pessimism of policy makers and social scientists. Ethnopolitical conflicts are caused and maintained by a multiplicity of subjective and structural forces that drive communities apart (Byrne and Carter 1996). However, a number of these so- called protracted ethnopolitical conflicts are on the road to a peaceful resolution (Sandole 1999). Peace building entails a long-term process of structural change and grassroots political, socioeconomic, and psychological empowerment (Lederach 1997). This book explores one possible mechanism of conflict transformation and peace building in post-ethnopolitical conflict—the role of external economic funding agencies in local economic development and inter-communal reconciliation in Northern Ireland—and addresses the role of economic assistance in the management and resolution of the protracted conflict in NI.

The research makes an important contribution to our understanding of how economic assistance impacts a divided society with a history of protracted violence. This is an underresearched area, and this work on NI could provide important perspectives of what could be called the idea of "peace through development." Moreover, the study contributes to our understanding of the role of external funding in sustainable economic development and peace building by reviewing the imagery of conflict and social change held by community group leaders, funding agency development officers, and civil servants. The process of postconflict peace building and economic aid in NI can be a model for other societies in transition to democracy—Afghanistan, Bosnia, Cyprus, East Timor, Iraq, Kosovo, Lebanon, Nicaragua, the Palestinian Authority, and South Africa—all attempting to heal and rebuild from the collective trauma of ethnopolitical violence. It is also important to be able to gauge the importance of NGOs and external funding agencies in providing an interdependent and collaborative context for the de-escalation of tensions and the adoption of positive peace building. It is possible that external economic assistance may promote a positive climate to induce cooperation across ethnic boundaries on superordinate economic goals that may spill over into cultural and political matters.

The Politics of the Peace Building Process in Northern Ireland

What can we learn from what these participants have to say about peace building in NI? As described above, the people interviewed for this study include civil servants, funding agency development officers, and community group leaders in Dublin, Derry, and the border area. Although these participants had different perspectives, they addressed common themes in their discussions. Some issues raised by the participants are social; others are political, economic, or ethical. The narratives and stories of the participants also reflect hope and a belief in the efforts of funding agencies to use economic resources to build local development and peace. In general, participants are of the opinion that the funding agencies support and sustain local efforts to forge a socioeconomic infrastructure that restores pride and responsibility in the socially excluded, as well as reducing support for political violence. Economic assistance has given them a psychological boost, making it possible for marginalized communities in the grass roots to promote employment, provide training, build capacity, and begin to facilitate cross-community relationships.

All of these respondents presented several different ideas about how external economic aid influences community rebuilding in NI. It is important to be aware that some of the interviewees may have magnified the consequences of economic assistance if they were receiving it, irrespective of its effects on the conflict. Some mentioned localism and personalism: "If you haven't got a government minister, you are way down the line in priority" (community group leader, Emmyvale).

Some mentioned that the civil servants administering the funding process did not understand the needs of local people: "The people who came down to interview or talk to you about your application generally aren't interested with the type of thing you're doing" (community group leader, Derry). As a result, some of the community group leaders felt that their applications were not considered because they did not put together a solid enough package to meet the criteria of either the IFI or EU Peace

I funding agency. In the "peace industry," as some community leaders call the process, it was perceived that those with the personal connections and who can use the bureaucratic jargon are awarded the funding. One must bear in mind that due to the intermeshing of political and socioeconomic forces, Protestants and Catholics compete for the same resources and for the same territory. This is the real political problem that decreases the effectiveness of economic aid.

Some mentioned the frustration of local communities: "It is extremely difficult to get money out of the system which means that groups on the ground get extremely frustrated" (community group leader, Derry). These respondents suggest that external economic assistance is not trickling down into marginalized areas. Protestant and Catholic working-class areas that have suffered the brunt of the Troubles are not seeing the kind of economic assistance necessary to kick-start local underdeveloped economies.

Some mentioned the wider political problem: "There is going to be a fair bit of sorting out to be done" (civil servant, Dublin). Hence, some respondents are leery that economic development was being substituted for real political change because contentious political issues needed to be resolved before deep reconciliation could take place between both communities. Economic self-interest, contact, and cooperation are not a panacea, and are insufficient reasons for the Unionist and Nationalist communities to want to work together. Old hatreds and suspicions remain entrenched within a bitterly divided and sectarian society so that forcing both communities to work together may in fact exacerbate and escalate the ethnic conflict.

As mentioned earlier, there was a concern from some respondents who perceived the peace process as a business and that when the funding ended, the voluntary groups would be the only ones remaining who would continue to work for peace, reconciliation, and economic development. For example, one of the community group leaders from Derry mentioned that a "peace industry" had emerged in response to the funding: "The analysis of the conflict here, which comes from the Peace and Reconciliation or Community Relations industry, is that this is a community conflict."

The most salient theme that emerged in talk about economic development and the funding agencies was the role of the bureaucracy. For example, a community group leader from Derrylin, Co. Fermanagh, articulated, "What I see is that there is too much bureaucracy, far too much of the money is wasted on pure administration." Others described tensions between community groups and the central and local bureaucracies, illuminating the unitary nature of both states that clash with the empowerment of grassroots citizens. Other participants' stories expressed concern over asymmetrical power differences and tensions between community groups, funding agencies, and local and central government as local groups begin to own the process, become more empowered, and challenge the status quo. These respondents suggest that bureaucratic control over the distribution and control of the funding process needs to be streamlined with fewer technical forms. They also suggest that the funds must not be used for government projects, and that more development officers are placed on the ground to work with the communities.

Several community group leaders linked their images of single-identity projects (working in one's own community rather than cross-community) to community development and conflict resolution. Some participants arguing for single-identity economic projects focused on the necessity of building up their own infrastructures so that reconciliation cannot be forced on the communities. Other participants argued that really deep reconciliation to promote a direct democracy and a shared civic culture was not taking place. Referring to the funding process, a community group leader from Derry said, "I think the baseline for moving to a point where there can be cross-community-led economic development is that individual communities on a single-identity basis need to be given the facilities and support and investment to be revitalized." Another community group leader from Derry spoke about the needs of each community: "You have got to understand your own culture first, and I believe that even understanding your own culture is a step forward toward understanding others." Thus, single identity is a pathway to community development, but perhaps more importantly, a process of building a community's self-esteem and self-efficacy, suggesting that the empowerment and political security of each community must come before the development of cross-community relationships. Indeed, without this, cross-community contact can reinforce sectarianism and stereotypical images of the other (Fitzduff 1996). The necessity of looking after one's own rather than cross-community interests is an enduring aspect of the bicommunal conflict in NI.

In Monaghan town, a development officer of an EU Peace I Fund agency expressed an emphatic image of getting money down to the grass roots. "I get out and work with the community to ensure that the money is put to good use." Interestingly, however, his perspective also points out that economic aid is tied to the wider politics and the peace process. "EU Peace and Reconciliation funding is but one part of a political solution." Other respondents believed that properly administered economic aid must be linked to a political settlement and structure that provides for inclusiveness and equality at all levels in the society.

In addition, a civil servant in Dublin described how the funding process has forged closer links between the agencies North and South of the border. "Every time that Mr. X goes out for a cup of coffee in Monaghan, he either ends up meeting people from the Peace Administration or IFI or the lay staff." Further, he said that both funding agencies are able to work closely together to prevent an overlap in projects. In this way, civil servants and the funding agencies can expedite projects quickly.

A community group leader from Derry said that economic development could change the way both communities relate to each other. "So, economic development is absolutely essential if it allows the people to come together." In addition, he articulated that economic cooperation would spill over into the political arena. "If you work for growth, the chances are that growth itself will lead to peace." Thus economic assistance properly administered may play a key role in fostering an environment conducive to the peaceful resolution of the NI conflict. Clearly, the respondents recognized the link between prosperity and the fact that peace is the end of the long war. However, Protestant Unionists do not perceive that the funds will build a lasting peace in NI. In the current climate Unionist mistrust of the peace process is indicative of mainstream Unionist uneasiness over the decommissioning of Republican and Loyalist arms. Prisoner release means less Unionist confidence in the GFA to resolve the conflict (Dixon 2000). It is within the Nationalist respondents that we see a belief in the positive role of the funding agencies in addressing economic disadvantage, and in reducing the levels of violence in NI. This finding is in contrast to the Unionists where there is minimal support for the idea that economic assistance can provide more economic opportunities and reduce the level of violence (Irvin and Byrne 2002). In general, Protestants find the distribution of the IFI and EU Peace I funds unfair. They perceive that Catholics are receiving all of the benefits of both funds.

Some of the participants' stories suggest that they believe that external economic funding has engendered community pride, self-esteem, and responsibility. As mentioned previously, socioeconomic development has given a psychological boost to rural areas and to communities along both sides of the Irish border. Some respondents argue that properly administered economic assistance is critical in empowering local communities to provide for their basic human needs and in rebuilding the infrastructure of NI and other ethnoterritorial conflicts recently ravaged by political violence.

Hence, agency funding (track eight) and government support (track one) has activated private citizens (track four) to economically regenerate relatively deprived communities within NI and the border area. Such an interactive intervention process demonstrates that multitrack intervention is a critical ingredient of peace building (Diamond and McDonald 1996). A multitrack systems approach brings together a myriad of perspectives, resources, and approaches that are necessary to deal with the intricate web of issues and parties that fuel ethnopolitical strife (Byrne and Keashly 2000). A multitrack diplomacy approach creates a mutual relationship built on trust, commitment, and partnership (Lederach 1997) to create a synergy between Unionists and Nationalists that empowers individual agency within the grass roots and community building that will transform values, perceptions, and structures within NI society.

Thus, commonsense economic policy strategies must be an integral part of an ethnic conflict resolution process that promotes economic growth and de-escalates economic tensions (Esman 1994, 1995, 1997). In NI, economic development alone is not a panacea to transform conflict between both communities. An intermeshing of socioeconomic and political forces that tear both communities apart must be addressed by a structure that builds peace in a collaborative and positive way (Byrne and Irvin 2000, 2001; Byrne and Ayulo 1998).

The respondents are of the opinion that properly targeted economic assistance can provide impoverished and marginalized members of both communities with material and human resources to build self-confidence and self-esteem in a nourishing milieu more conducive to political rather than violent solutions to conflict, resulting in the end of both the war economy and poverty. Nationalist and Republican respondents clearly believe that economic assistance has made a decisive difference in targeting poverty within the Catholic community. Peace brings prosperity. The data also indicates that skills and training are needed to assist the Loyalist and Republican paramilitaries to reintegrate peacefully into their communities as well as retraining those employed in the security forces for postconflict job opportunities. However, moderate Nationalist and Unionist politicians remain intransigent and deadlocked over the decommissioning of paramilitary weapons, alarmed about paramilitary punishment beatings, criminal activity, and low-level sectarian violence (such as the January 30, 2005, murder of Robert McCartney from the Short Strand area of Belfast), and are concerned about PIRA's involvement in the December 23, 2004, Northern Bank robbery of UK£26 million.

The same hopes aroused by the peace process culminating in the 1998 Good Friday Agreement have promised to usher in an economic and political environment, bringing peace and prosperity to the people of NI. Expectations were raised by the initial successful progress of the peace process. However, the unemployment rate remains high. Institution-building measures and economic policies need to be implemented by both governments to accelerate private and public investment to support and strengthen the work nurtured by both the IFI and the EU Peace I funds to reignite the microenterprise sector in deprived working-class neighborhoods. An already weak productive base in NI must be bolstered by economic policies that encourage economic growth and development policies that empower the entrepreneurial spirit of both working-class communities. Development policies must not be perceived by either community as another tool of British subvention and control or they would indeed reescalate tensions between Protestants and Catholics.

The research findings indicate the necessity of taking the role of economic factors in relation to sociopolitical and psychocultural factors into account in future policy making—looking at the advantages of certain economic policies and ways of implementing/delivering such policies to both communities. Politics has been far more important than economics in resolving and transforming NI's conflict over the past thirty years. What separates the current peace process from the period of protracted violence (1969–94) is, after all, not a change in economic investment in the region, or a change in the region's economic well-being, but a political settlement in the shape of the 1998 GFA, which has, at its center, a comprehensive range of new political power-sharing institutions as well as efforts to engage grassroots citizens. This point is borne out by Unionist respondents in this study who believe that politics—not economics—is what counts in the process to end the violence in NI. In a recent study of a randomly selected sample of one thousand respondents, findings indicate that there is a general disillusionment with the 1998 GFA within the Unionist community who highlight North–South bodies, reform of the police, and power-sharing institutions as critical concerns (Dowds, Hayes, and McAllister 2005)

Economic aid can lead to corruption if it falls into the wrong hands, and there is a substantial literature on this (Brown 2001; Licklider 2001). Within the context of NI, some have also argued that economic assistance encourages irresponsibility; that is, it shelters intransigent political actors from the economic consequences of their intractable attitudes (Darby 2001; Dixon 2000). The large British subvention to the region helped prevent a settlement for thirty years, as living standards were maintained at a reasonably high level irrespective of high levels of political extremism and violence (Bew, Patterson, and Gibbon 2002; McGarry and O'Leary 1995). Economic aid/assistance must be tied to political progress that combines the power-sharing approach with engaging people in the grass roots to be active participants in the building of civic society.

FUTURE RESEARCH POSSIBILITIES

A Multitrack Intervention Approach

The respondents in this study articulate that economic aid on its own is not a panacea; a political conflict demands a political solution. With government peace agreements currently under fire in NI and their continued inability to sustain peace over time, there is some possibility that current peace models focused solely on the capacity of one political organizational level to effect change (i.e., government) may be inadequate. Increasingly there is a growing sense among peace practitioners and researchers that some of the so-called modern strategies for conflict resolution are remote from the people whom they aim to assist and tend to be expensive strategies for intervention and mediation (Byrne and Irvin 2000; Lederach 1997).

Moreover, culture is also an important component and resource in conflict analysis and resolution (Avruch 1998; Augsburger 1992; Ross 1993). Culture is rooted in sound knowledge. For example, indigenous methods seek methodologies that create an encounter between people in a given setting and their own rich understanding of conflict and how to intervene in conflict (Tuso 2000). Basically, indigenous mechanisms are closely tied to grassroots peacemaking approaches that presuppose that it is possible to build peace from below (Ury, Brett, and Goldberg 1993; Lederach 1997).

In societies of violent, protracted conflict, peace cannot be realized or sustained without the significant involvement of grassroots community initiatives, nongovernmental community-based organizations, and government working in partnership to repair harm, transform relationships, and restore peace (Paffenholz and Reychler 2005). Such a process involves conflict resolution and peace building in their interpersonal, professional, cultural, and political dimensions, and calls upon different resolution theories, techniques, and analytical tools.

Consequently, a multitrack intervention approach is needed that reflects the variety of civil society activities initiated and sustained by a broad range of actors, including, among others, political elites, women's groups, youth groups, elderly groups, faith-based organizations, economic leaders, community organizers, teachers, and health care workers (Van Tongeren, Hellema, and Verhoeven 2005). This inclusive, holistic, interdisciplinary, and proactive approach to peace building allows initiative, creativity, and imagination to flourish across these tracks—transforming real and pressing political problems in real and constructive ways.

Traditional peace-building models such as consociational power sharing (Byrne 2001a; Lijphart 1977; Pearson 2001) and civil-society approaches (Dixon 1997; Kriesberg 1998) have tended to focus on the position and resources of one particular level of policy making (i.e., government) in effecting change. Some conflict resolution researchers suggest that this conceptual work has failed to address the critical relationships between grassroots communities, midlevel community-based organizations, and the politico-governmental elite in building a comprehensive peacemaking model (Jeong 2005; Lederach 1997). Such an integrated peace-building model would arguably be central to sustaining long-term peace in places of sustained violence such as NI (Dixon 1997; O'Leary and McGarry 1993; Wright 1987).

For example, Lederach (1997) describes a three-tiered peace-building model consisting, at the highest level, of high-visibility socioeconomic and political leadership (i.e., religious and military). This would be followed at the next level by academics, ethnic, professional, and religious leaders, as well as large-scale or well-known nongovernmental organizations, and a third level that includes grassroots local leaders and the citizenry who experience, from a survivalist perspective, the quotidian effects of consistent, front-line, violent conflict. Lederach argues that the importance of the middle level, which provides a critical structural and organizational link between the top and bottom rungs, is typically neglected in designing and implementing peace initiatives. In the case of NI, the integrative potential of middle-tier leaders and organizations to communicate between political leadership and grassroots organizers has been underutilized (Byrne 2001b). Moreover, the uniqueness, interdependency, and legitimacy of both the needs and resources of the grass roots, middle range, and top level have been systematically misunderstood or ignored (Lederach 1997).

Moreover, Lederach (1999b) cites the need for interdisciplinary approaches to peace building by integrating theories of conflict transformation, health care, politics, and socioeconomic development. Experience shows a highly interdependent relationship among these conceptual perspectives, yet the degree to which current practices reflect this perspective remains unclear. Integrating Lederach's (1997, 1999a) inclusive multitrack peace model with other practical approaches provides for a more comprehensive conceptual model that would better characterize key relationships between government, midrange, and grassroots levels in the peace process. It is important to mobilize government-community partnerships (Byrne 2001a, 2001b).

As part of a multitrack intervention approach, the United Nations (UN) could, for example, develop an international alert system to watch for early warning signs of escalation in protracted ethnic conflict milieus. For example, a proposed NGO called Ethnowatch could follow local newspapers and media to monitor trigger factors such as ideology, a change in political rhetoric or demographics, a decline in intermarriage, and the outbreak of violence (Byrne and Keashly 2000). Such early warning indicators on the ground would provide invaluable information for policy makers, third-party mediators, NGOs, the UN peacekeepers or blue helmets, and the Security Council, so they could intervene to prevent the escalation of ethnopolitical conflict (Keashly and Fisher 1996). On the ground, use of video cameras to collect data, plus a field survey of NGO workers in the Red Cross, Doctors Without Borders, and War Child among others, would provide important indicators of possible outbreaks of violence.

In addition, a mechanism could be put in place in NI to liaise with those groups engaged in the funding and delivery of economic assistance programs. A conference/forum for donors, policy makers, and representatives of various bodies engaged and involved in the delivery of economic assistance could be undertaken with a local partner (local universities and/or an independent think tank such as Democratic Dialogue) that would help to translate these research findings into useful guidelines for the wider peace-building community. In this way a project that studies peace building could also contribute significantly to peace building in NI. Questions could be asked; for example, who are the key figures and organizations to be targeted for future funding in NI and along the Irish border area?

Ethnic Conflict Transformation, Sustainable Economic Aid, and Peace Building

ETHNIC LEADERSHIP

Poor economic conditions have exacerbated competition and tension between local ethnic communities that have exploded into intercommunal violence. Dominant ethnic group leaders have played the ethnic card in their dealings with minority communities, making sure that citizenship, language, religion, schooling, housing, employment, and government representation remain firmly within the purview of their community (Gurr 2000). Deprivation, discontent, and alienation within the subordinate community have escalated into ethnopolitical violence as their ethnic majority leaders manipulate the economic structure for personal interests (Pearson 2001). Consequently, majority community leaders must exercise restraint in promising immediate economic prosperity. By offering instead the realistic promise of slow economic growth, they will not raise unrealistic expectations that could detonate into ethnic violence if and when the subordinate group is scapegoated for the economic woes of the state (Esman 1997). Ethnic group leaders must educate and expand public awareness about the reality of that state's economic situation. They must realize that long-term intercommunal violence will seriously damage the infrastructure of the state, impact the level of private investment and tourism, and ensure that the best and the brightest move elsewhere (ibid.).

Ethnic conflict transformation, therefore, must be the ultimate economic policy goal of external funding agencies and majoritarian governments (Esman 1997). External funding agencies and governments must painstakingly build conflict resolution, peace building, and social justice measures into sustainable development packages that ensure the equal distribution of economic resources across all communities. "Peace is most commonly found where economic growth and opportunities to share in that growth are broadly distributed across the population" (Carnegie Commission 1997, xxxii). For example, the conciliatory leadership approach of Nelson Mandela created a unified rainbow coalition approach to economic problems that a new South Africa now faces. Ethnic group leaders in Afghanistan, Bosnia, Cyprus, East Timor, Iraq, Kosovo, NI, the Palestinian Authority, and Sri Lanka among others could do well to model Nelson Mandela's inclusive political behavior and "walk the talk" that also promoted sustainable development as an important mechanism of conflict transformation (Ryan 1996). Incorporating civil and political liberties, the voice of grassroots citizens could go a long way to ensure the growth and viability of each of these region's economies (Esman 1997).

CIVIL SOCIETY APPROACH

Responding to local needs, governments and funding agencies must create a grant application process whereby community groups need not compromise their aims and goals to fit the priorities and interests of funding NGOs. This NI case study clearly illustrates this point. To promote true grassroots participatory democracy and enhance effective communication and information sharing across both communities, the criteria of both the IFI and the EU Peace I funds must be simplified. True sustainable development, as a critical element of transformational ethnic conflict resolution, will de-escalate structural violence, improve socioeconomic conditions, and facilitate a just political system to develop that will prevent the emergence of protracted ethnopolitical conflict. Building sustainable peace and social justice requires a grassroots communitarian approach that reflects the worldviews of and develops constructive relationships within and between communities, governments, and NGOs in the construction of a proactive civil society (Lederach 2005).

Consequently, by addressing the systemic roots of conflict in order to produce a culture of peace (Byrne 2001a, 2001b; Dixon 1997; Kriesberg 1998), the civil society approach encourages relationship building and development of intergroup trust. The model focuses directly on citizen participation made manifest, for example, through cultural traditions initiatives, integrated education, and education for mutual understanding initiatives (Byrne 2001a). However, civil society models tend to minimize the importance of political power brokering and overestimate the impact of community-based and grassroots initiatives on citizen behavior (Kriesberg 1998). A shortcoming of this model is that it neglects the importance of government position and resource mobilization in effecting peace.

Transformative Conflict Resolution and Third-Party Intervention

MIDDLE-TIER ELITES

The transformational approach to peace building also recognizes the integrative potential of middle-tier elites in influencing ethnic decision makers and the grass roots (Lederach 1997). Third-party intermediaries in a postconflict peace-building model must seek a real transformation of such underlying impediments to peace as distrust, bitterness, insecurity, institutional failure, economic dislocation, and normative dissension. Even in situations like Israel and the Palestinian Authority, East Timor, and Sri Lanka, where formal peacekeeping has either broken down or not yet been tried, there is a need for elements of transformation just to get beyond the fighting. Third parties can contribute to successful conflict resolution by acting to defuse violence, to protect borders and groups, to provide outside funding and resources, and to promote a balance of power among adversaries (Lederach 1997). On the other hand, outside parties can exacerbate conflict and promote violence by supplying fuel for the fighting in the form of resources to aligned internal protagonists as in Cyprus and Sierra Leone (Byrne 2000).

Middle-tier elites can help to create and implement a vision of peace that promotes intergroup relations by addressing subjective and objective issues among decision makers and the grass roots (Lederach 1997). Moreover, middle-tier elites can facilitate direct democracy by promoting, through a holistic model of cooperation and collaboration (Woolpert, Slaton, and Schwerin 1998; Miall, Ramsbotham, and Woodhouse 1999) the social and political responsibilities of each citizen to helping others while empowering themselves. In the past, third-party intervention in ethnopolitical conflict has focused on the management or microanalysis of such disputes (Dukes 1996; Princen 1991). Today, the transformative practice of ethnopolitical conflict resolution seeks to change traditional practices of institutions, government agencies, and communities contributing to the capacity of powerless groups to determine their own destinies relative to the common good of the overall society (Lederach 1997).

Transformational conflict resolution focuses on the means of changing structures, institutions, substantive issues, and relationships to build a just and sustainable culture of peace. This entails an inclusive, participatory, nonviolent, and evolutionary process that acknowledges and respects differences and encourages cooperation among groups engaged in pro- tracted intercommunal conflict (Byrne and Keashly 2000). Protracted conflicts are carried on by both elites and masses in a society, and some- times perpetuated by outside interveners (Pearson 2001). Hence, trans- formation processes can, and some would argue, must be approached from the elite level of authoritative decisions and policy reforms, the popular level of group and interpersonal interaction and bargaining, and the regional or international level to foster restraint and support of an incubation process for the evolving political accommodation (Lederach 1997; Sandole 1999). For example, instead of putting clear and sepa- rate issues on the table, negotiators might express interests that represent complex underlying needs such as security, territory, identity, recogni- tion, and resources (Burton 1990; Volkan 1998).

However, elite-level bargaining might not be sufficient to produce lasting terms of settlement if the general public and the ultras within minorities do not accept the accords. There would be a need for interac- tive conflict resolution, that is, the involvement of popular organizations in the bargaining and mutual encounters, common action projects, and dialogues (Fisher 1996, 2005). Local people are the creators of their own knowledge and use an elictive approach in managing conflict, sometimes based an insider partial model of mediation that is in turn sustained by an already established system of peacemaking (Lederach 1995) or tra- ditional practices modified for the developing circumstances. Whether reconciliation comes through restorative justice approaches as in South Africa (the Truth and Reconciliation Commission) or through exten- sive social dialogue, storytelling (Senehi 2000; Senehi and Byrne 2006), encounter groups, or joint action projects (such as Project Children and Seeds for Peace), the assumption is that there must be a deepening of understanding and mutual responsiveness that goes beyond mere negoti- ated agreements.

I believe sustainable development has an important role to play as a psycho-socioeconomic and political component of communitarian eth- nic conflict resolution and that more research is needed to explore that connection. As ethnopolitical conflict enters a peace-building stage in Bosnia, Cyprus, East Timor, Iraq, Kosovo, NI, Rwanda, Sri Lanka, and South Africa, empirical research needs to focus on the possible roles of foreign aid, inside and outside mediators, and NGOs as important

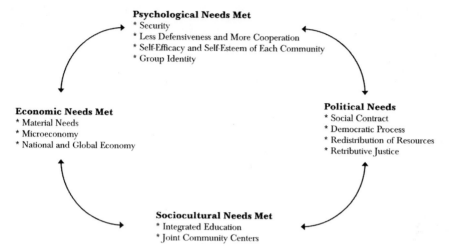

Figure 1. Components of Psycho-Socioeconomic and Political Sustainability and Human Development

structural building blocs in these conflicts. It is necessary to determine whether economic intervention in such conflicts contributes to the ability of all ethnic communities to achieve human goals and basic human needs (Burton 1990). If we are to create and sustain the kind of world where ethnic conflict becomes a thing of the past, there must be an understanding of the connection between sustainable socioeconomic development and ethnic conflict resolution as well as how it contributes to the goals of social justice and transformation.

PEACE BUILDING AND RECONCILIATION

Ethnic conflict is experienced and sustained in networks of relationships. The findings from this study underscore the necessity of understanding how past conflict can be used to forge empowering relationships between ethnic groups. A process of reconciliation whereby accountability, acknowledgment, apology, contrition, forgiveness, justice, mercy, and peace are built into the peace-building process can positively reconstruct the relationship so that ethnic groups can coexist and conclude the conflict peacefully (Arthur 2000).

Political agreements that are solution-oriented do not resolve ethnopolitical conflict nor provide sustainable peaceful relations. A process of reconciliation is needed, not merely to resolve political issues (Lederach 2002), but to restore relationships. Underlying fear and mistrust require a deep-rooted process of reconciliation to prevent the future recycling of violence and conflict (Ackermann 2000, 2003; Appleton 2005; Irani and

Funk 2001) and to transform socioeconomic and political structures still laden with an acceptable level of violence (Galtung 1996).

As ethnic groups make choices, take risks, and open up to learning to search for constructive engagements and conclusions to ethnic conflicts (Appleton 2005), acknowledgment and remembrance of past humiliation, oppression, and shame is critical to ensure compassion and justice in the present for the sake of a peaceful future. Third-party dialogue, as part of a multimodal process to transform the complexity of relationships and interactions (Botes 2003; Byrne and Keashly 2000), can also help to transform personal and social relations. As the groups move toward acknowledgment of authentic accountability, apology, compensation, and forgiveness, all parties must pursue a mutual recognition and reconciliation that insures human rights and safeguards and establishes truth, justice, peace, and mercy (Appleton 2005; Lederach 1997). Moreover, "decoupling intergroup relations" (single identity within the NI context), builds autonomy and self-reliance and may be essential for a certain period of time "to build a healthy coping that enhances the self-agency of the ethnic group to reconstruct a reconciliatory relationship based on trust" (Appleton 2005, 192).

In this process, constructive storytelling is critical to building inner and cross-community peace because it carves out critical spaces for ethnopolitical groups to "create, recreate and alter social identities, power relations, knowledge, memory and emotion" (Senehi 2000, 97, cited in Appleton 2005, 203). Constructive storytelling offers a multidimensional umbrella to ethnopolitical groups for reconciliation that involves negotiating powerful relationships within and among community groups (Senehi 2000, 2002). Constructive stories expose the painful truth, allowing both ethnic groups the critical space to construct a shared interpretation of the past in order to come to terms with the past (Appleton 2005; Senehi and Byrne 2006), to end the transgenerational transmission of trauma and time collapse (Volkan 1998), and to build trust and a coactive power (Kriesberg 2002; Minow 1998; Tutu 1999) in a constructive conflict interaction. Thus, a "mutual conciliatory accommodation" is developed that acknowledges what happened, redresses past injustices, builds economic infrastructures, and anticipates mutual human and collective security and well-being (Appleton 2005). Consequently, research needs to be directed at the sociopolitical process of economic assistance in concert with relational transformation and reconciliation.

Project Evaluation and Assessment

As international donor agencies have become increasingly involved in post-conflict peace building, there has evolved a greater awareness of the fact that the economic policies that have exacerbated cultural, socioeconomic, and political cleavages have been identified as significant causes of the violent civil wars and their remedy a key component in postconflict peace building. To date, however, most studies of international peace-building assistance programs have focused on issues of delivery, distribution, and product (Paffenholz 2000, 2005; Paffenholz and Reychler 2005). This literature is both uneven in scope and very compartmentalized, with history and politics being far more extensively addressed than conflict resolution and peace studies. Indeed, as Lederach (1997) notes, relatively few studies have been produced that examine postconflict peace-building issues in relationship to the socioeconomic and political context (18).

Susan Allen Nan (2005) suggests that a holistic peacemaking system includes modes of cooperative interaction between track one diplomacy (official, governmental) and track two diplomacy (unofficial, nongovernmental). Further, Allen-Nan argues that conflict resolution initiatives addressing international conflicts must be seriously considered in an intervention process. These would include: (1) communication, where information is shared by all parties to build good working relationships, (2) coordination, to synchronize interventions in the peace process, (3) cooperation, to share resources and prevent overlap, and (4) collaboration, to ensure successful joint initiatives. In a similar vein, Paffenholz and Reychler (2005) propose a comprehensive multipurpose and multilevel approach that facilitates the planning, analysis, evaluation, and assessment of peace, as well as economic assistance interventions that take place in the aftermath of protracted ethnic conflict and/or in latent and manifest violent conflicts. Such a holistic and inclusive transformational process involves all citizens as active participants in the constructive process of peace building. For example, a multidimensional or social cubism approach that considers ethnopolitical conflict as a multifaceted puzzle of six interrelated forces—demographics, economics, history, politics, psychoculture, and history—can provide a complete picture of the dynamics that shape conflict and its resolution in NI (Byrne and Carter 1996).

A conceptual framework for building peace that links together various aspects and dimensions of peace building must address, therefore, the underlying and interrelated structural and psychocultural forces that exacerbate ethnopolitical conflict (Diamond and McDonald 1996; Byrne and Keashly 2000). For example, positional dialogue between political elites is assisting parties to focus on the immediate cessation of political violence (McGarry 1998). Middle-tier elites and NGOs are attempting to create a sustainable infrastructure using a multimodal and multilevel contingency approach to the peace processes (Byrne and Keashly 2000). External economic assistance from public and private sources is addressing structural inequalities in NI by stimulating sustainable economic development in neighborhoods with a history of chronic unemployment, thus deescalating intergroup competition for economic resources (Byrne and Ayulo 1998; Byrne and Irvin 2000, 2001). Finally, middle-tier elites and conflict resolution professionals are using dialogue groups, problem-solving workshops, and storytelling to facilitate constructive interaction in critical spaces so that participants can learn to challenge belief structures that can help in the process of creating structural change, and in creating a vision of a desired future (Fisher 1996; Kelman 1997; Rothman 1997; Senehi 2000, 2002).

However, contact is not enough; for the outcomes of peace building, the international donors and policy makers need to look at structural change. Allen Nan (2005) suggests that peace building has two functions: (1) building structures of peace, and (2) the deconstruction of structures of violence. Indicators need to be developed by donors and policy makers at the micro- and macrolevels as to how economic assistance has impacted on the peace process. Allen Nan (2005), Paffenholz (2000, 2005), and Snyder (2005) suggest that a number of important questions need to be asked. Has reconciliation been reached? Has the development dimension impacted the power structure to nurture capacities for peace? Who is coordinating the planning, intervention, and evaluation of the implementation of the peace-building process? Has the intervention's objectives and activities met local needs, goals, and visions? What are the monitoring systems indicators that demonstrate the impacts, outcomes, outputs, and activities of economic aid intervention on the overall peace process? How is the community-based bottom-up approach to peace building and the empowerment of civil society complementing track one (political diplomacy) approaches? Is the peace-building process sustainable and flexible enough to meet new socioeconomic and political challenges? Are tensions created where the aid is going? How do donors, policy makers, development officers, and the grass roots conceptualize economic development, peace building, and the politics of civic society? How do donors integrate these concepts into the planning, assessment, and implementation stage of its peace-building strategy? Can NGOs be used as a bridge between the ethnic groups to build intergroup relationships (that addresses past and future relationships), capacity building, and trust? I believe this study has at least begun to address and to answer some of these important questions.

CONCLUSIONS

Economic donors with properly targeted aid, in conjunction with other intervention tracks (i.e., the political process), can assist parties to forge a holistic and inclusive transformational process that involves all citizens as active participants in the constructive process of peace building. The 1998 GFA promises a brighter future for all groups in NI who are attempting to transform relationships between antagonists and to institutionalize a peace-building infrastructure. The Belfast Agreement and the recent power-sharing government at Stormont suggest that, for now, the conflict in NI is in a downward spiral. In this process of de-escalation, sustainable psycho-socioeconomic and political development may be the most critical aspects of peace building in a region that, for thirty years, was racked by ethnopolitical strife. While both the IFI and EU Peace I funding agencies are working to reignite the entrepreneurial economic spirit in local communities, for now it seems that the Protestant and Catholic communities are mainly looking inward to kick-start their own individual community economies and political infrastructure rather than embracing, in a substantial way, socioeconomic rebuilding on a cross-community basis. The challenge will be to develop indigenous capitalist models to generate greater interdependence between both communities, that is, projects that require cross-community trading and the manufacturing of products.

This focus on single community issues and identity may be a necessary first step to developing self-awareness, self-esteem, and self-efficacy. In turn, the empowerment of each community will create a better cross-community dialogue and a working relationship that will lead to the accommodation of both ethnocultures. The rapid growth of the Celtic Tiger economy in the Republic of Ireland will also ensure that it is within the interest of elites in NI to cooperate with elites in Southern Ireland on common superordinate politico-economic goals. Sustainable psycho-socioeconomic and political development will be congruent with changing socioeconomic and cultural regions within a Europe of the Regions (Byrne 1995).

We must continue to explore the impact of sustainable socioeconomic aid and NGOs on the structural economic and political inequalities within ethnopolitical conflicts. Economic policy goals must be built into an ethnic conflict resolution model that seeks to transform subjective and objective factors that drive ethnic groups into divided individualist communities. Sustainability must be based on a holistic systems perspective that exemplifies and clarifies not only the interdependent relationship between NGOs, groups, communities, and states, but also the processes that exist and flow between them. Socioeconomic problems must not be divorced from political issues. Instead, a transformative peace-building approach must involve citizens, political and economic elites, and funding agencies to work together to develop joint strategies to address common problems and develop a mutual relationship. Only then can a just and positive peace be created so that an interdependent society can grow together in NI.

During the ensuing thirty years of the Troubles, NI generated the most intense political violence within any region of the EU and in the liberal states of post–World War II (O'Leary and McGarry 1993, 8). In addition, the consociational, elite power-sharing political accommodation model embodied in the current GFA has not created a deferential mass in NI willing to accept such cosponsored peace initiatives (Byrne 2001a, 2001b; Dixon 1997; O'Leary and McGarry 1993). This approach has tended to overemphasize short-term tasks and concerns, such as decommissioning in NI, which tend to be separated from the long-range social change goals needed to bolster any macropolitical achievements made (Knox and Quirk 2000, 24). Thus, initial positive signs may have given way to stalemate, intransigence, and unwillingness to compromise. There is a danger that the early euphoria of ending the strife may not be sustained by politicians who find it difficult to negotiate their group's basic needs—identity, security, recognition, and resources. The provision for disarmament of the PIRA and Loyalist paramilitaries continues to be a hotly contested issue in the formal negotiations and agreements. And yet, as both communities continue to struggle with the legacy of the conflict, the 1998 GFA and the economic assistance from the IFI and the EU Peace I Fund provide hope for the future as both communities continue to struggle with the legacy of the conflict. Respondents in the study suggest that for both funds to be more effective and deliver aid more appropriately, both funders must streamline the bureaucracy and include peace-building and capacity-building criteria that reflect local needs rather than the funders' strategic interests. Northern Ireland could become an important model of success for other societies transitioning out of violent conflict.

Works Cited

Ackermann, A. 2000. *Making peace prevail: Preventing violent conflict in Macedonia.* Syracuse, NY: Syracuse University Press.

———. The idea and practice of conflict prevention. *Journal of Peace Research* 40(3): 339–47.

Agnew, J. 1989. Beyond reason: Spatial and temporal sources of ethnic conflicts. In *Intractable conflicts and their transformation,* edited by L. Kriesberg, T. A. Northrup, and S. J. Thorson, 41–53. Syracuse, NY: Syracuse University Press.

Agnew, J., and S. Corbridge. 1994. *Mastering space: Hegemony, territory and international political economy.* New York: Routledge.

Allen Nan, S. 2005. Modes of track one–track two cooperation in conflict resolution. Forty-eighth Annual International Studies Association Convention. Honolulu, Hawaii.

Amin, S. 1997. *Capitalism in the age of globalization: The management of contemporary society.* London: Zed Books.

Anderson, M. B. 1999. *Do no harm: How aid can support peace or war.* Boulder, CO: Lynne Rienner.

Anglo Irish Agreement. 1985. Dublin: Iveagh House.

Appleton, C. 2005. Playing with fire: The meaning of reconciling. Doctoral Dissertation, Department of Conflict Analysis and Resolution, Graduate School of Humanities and Social Sciences, Nova Southeastern University, Florida.

Arthur, P. 2000. *Special relationships: Britain, Ireland, and Northern Ireland.* Belfast: Blackstaff Press.

Augsburger, D. W. 1992. *Conflict mediation across cultures: Pathways and patterns.* Westminster: John Knox Press.

Avruch, K. 1998. *Culture and conflict resolution.* Washington, DC: United States Institute of Peace Press.

Bercovitch, J., ed. 1996. *Resolving international conflicts: The theory and practice of mediation.* Boulder, CO: Lynne Rienner.

Berdal, M., and D. M. Malone. 2000. *Greed and grievance: Economic agendas in civil wars.* Boulder, CO: Lynne Rienner.

Bew, P. 2007. *Ireland: The politics of enmity, 1789–2006.* Oxford: Oxford University Press.

Bew, P., and H. Patterson. 1985. *The British state and the Ulster crisis: From Wilson to Thatcher.* London: Verso.

Bew, P., P. Gibbon, and H. Patterson. 1979. *The state in Northern Ireland, 1921–72: Political forces and social classes.* Manchester: Manchester University Press.

———. 1995. *Northern Ireland, 1921–1994: Political forces and social classes.* London: Serif.

———. 2002. *Northern Ireland, 1921–2001: Political forces and social classes.* Northampton, MA: Interlink.

Bogdan, R., and S. Biklin. 1992. *Qualitative research for education: An introduction to theory and methods.* Needham Heights, MA: Allyn and Bacon.

Botes, J. 2003. Conflict transformation: A debate over semantics or a crucial shift in the theory and practice of peace and conflict studies? *International Journal of Peace Studies* 8(2): 1–27.

Boulding, E. 1990. *Building a global civic culture: Education for an interdependent world.* Syracuse, NY: Syracuse University Press.

———. 2000. *Cultures of peace: The hidden side of history.* Syracuse, NY: Syracuse University Press.

Boyce, J. K., and M. O'Donnell, eds. 2007. *Peace and the public purse: Economic policies for postwar statebuilding.* Boulder, CO: Lynne Rienner.

———. 2005. Development assistance, conditionality and war economies. In *Profiting from peace: Managing the resource dimension of civil war,* edited by Karen Ballentine and Heiko Nitzschke, 287–314. Boulder, CO: Lynne Rienner.

Boyce, J. K. 2000. Beyond good intentions: External assistance and peace building. In *Good intentions: Pledges of aid for post conflict recovery,* edited by S. Forman and S. Patrick, 367–82. Boulder, CO: Lynne Rienner.

Boyle, K., and T. Hadden. 1994. *Northern Ireland: The choice.* London: Penguin.

Brett, C. E. B. 1990. The International Fund for Ireland, 1986–1989. *Political Quarterly* 61(1): 425–49.

Brown, M. E. 2001. Ethnic and internal conflicts: Causes and implications. In *Turbulent peace: The challenges of managing international conflict,* edited by C. Crocker, F. Osler Hampson, and P. Aall, 209–26. Washington, DC: United States Institute of Peace Press.

Bruce, S. 1986. *God save Ulster: The religion and politics of Paisleyism.* Oxford: Clarendon Press.

Brynen, R. 2000. *A very political economy: Peace building and foreign aid in the West Bank and Gaza.* Washington, DC: United States Institute of Peace Press.

———. 2005. Donor assistance: Lessons from Palestine for Afghanistan. In *Postconflict development: Meeting new challenges,* edited by G. June and W. Verkoren, 223–48. Boulder, CO: Lynne Rienner.

Buchanan, S. 2005. Cost of conflict, price of peace: Conflict transformation through social and economic development. PhD dissertation, Department of Politics, University of Ulster-Coleraine.

Burton, J. 1987. *Resolving deep-rooted conflict.* Lanham, MD: University Press of America.

———. 1990. *Conflict: Resolution and provention theory.* London: Macmillan.

Byrne, S. 1995. Conflict regulation or conflict resolution: Third-party intervention in the Northern Ireland conflict; Prospects for peace. *Terrorism and Political Violence* 7(2): 1–24.

———. 1997. *Growing up in a divided society: The influence of conflict on Belfast schoolchildren.* Madison, NJ: Fairleigh Dickinson University Press.

———. 1999. Northern Ireland, Israel, and South Africa at a crossroads: Understanding intergroup conflict, peace-building, and conflict resolution. *International Journal of Group Tensions* 28(3): 231–53.

———. 2000. Power politics as usual in Cyprus and Northern Ireland: Divided islands and the roles of external ethno-guarantors. *Nationalism and Ethnic Politics* 6(1): 1–24.

————. 2001a. Transformational conflict resolution and the Northern Ireland conflict. *International Journal on World Peace* 27(2): 3–22.

————. 2001b. Consociational and civic society approaches to peace building in Northern Ireland. *Journal of Peace Research* 38(3): 327–52.

————. 2002. Toward tractability: The 1993 South African Record of Understanding and the 1998 Northern Ireland Good Friday Agreement. *Irish Studies in International Affairs* 13(1): 135–49.

————. 2007. Mired in intractability: The roles of external ethno-guarantors and primary mediators in Cyprus and Northern Ireland. *Conflict Resolution Quarterly* 24(2): 149–72.

Byrne, S., and N. Carter. 1996. Social cubism: Six social forces of ethnoterritorial politics in Northern Ireland and Quebec. *Peace and Conflict Studies* 3(2): 52–72.

Byrne, S., and M. Ayulo. 1998. External economic aid in ethno-political conflict: A view from Northern Ireland. *Security Dialogue* 29(4): 219–33.

Byrne, S., and A. Delman. 1999. Identity, ideology and intragroup conflict: The effect of high impact conflict on Lubavitch and Liberal Jews in Ft. Lauderdale and Protestant and Catholic schoolchildren in Belfast. *Journal of Intergroup Relations* 25(4): 35–58.

Byrne, S., and C. Irvin, eds. 2000. *Reconcilable differences: Turning points in ethno-political conflict.* West Hartford, CT: Kumarian.

————. 2001. Economic aid and policymaking: Building the peace dividend in Northern Ireland. *Policy and Politics* 29(1): 413–29.

————. 2002. A shared common sense: Perceptions of the material effects and impacts of economic growth in Northern Ireland. *Civil Wars* 5(1): 55–86.

Byrne, S., and L. Keashly. 2000. Working with ethno-political conflict: A multi-modal and multi-level approach to conflict intervention. *International Peacekeeping* 7(1): 97–120.

Byrne, S., N. Carter, and J. Senehi. 2003. Social cubism and social conflict: Analysis and resolution. *Journal of International and Comparative Law* 8(3): 725–40.

Byrne, S., C. Irvin, E. Fissuh, and C. Cunningham. 2006. People's perceptions of the role of economic assistance in conflict reduction in Northern Ireland. *Peace and Conflict Studies* 13(2): 1–21.

Byrne, S., D. Sandole, I. Sandole-Starosta, and J. Senehi, eds. 2008. *Handbook of conflict analysis and resolution.* Abingdon, Oxford: Routledge.

Callaghan, W. S. 1983. Report on proceedings first public session, New Ireland Forum. Dublin: Irish Stationery Office.

Caradosa, F. H., and E. Faletto. 1979. *Dependency and development in Latin America.* Berkeley: University of California Press.

Carment, D., and P. James, eds. 1997. *Wars in the midst of peace: The international politics of ethnic conflict.* Pittsburgh: University of Pittsburgh Press.

Carnegie Commission on Preventing Deadly Conflict. 1997. *Preventing deadly conflict.* Washington, DC: Carnegie Corporation of New York.

Chubb, B. 1992. *The government and politics of Ireland.* New York: Longman.

Coakley, J. 1996. The foundations of statehood. In *Politics in the Republic of Ireland*, edited by J. Coakley and M. Gallagher, 3–35. London: Routledge.

Cohen, R. 1999. *Negotiating across cultures: International communication in an interdependent world.* Washington, DC: United States Institute of Peace Press.

Comerford, V. 2003. *Ireland: Inventing the nation.* London: Arnold.

Coopers and Lybrand. 1997. Special support program for peace and reconciliation in Northern Ireland and the Border Counties of Ireland, 1995–1999. Midterm evaluation final report. Belfast.

Cousens, E. M., C. Kumar, and K. Wermester, eds. 2000. *Peace building as politics: Cultivating peace in fragile societies.* Boulder, CO: Lynne Rienner.

Cox, M. 1999. The war that came in from the cold: Clinton and the Irish question. *World Policy* 16(1): 53–75.

Cox, M., A. Guelke, and F. Stephen. 2000. Introduction: A farewell to arms? From long war to uncertain peace in Northern Ireland. In *A farewell to arms? From "long war" to long peace in Northern Ireland,* edited by M. Cox, A. Guelke, and F. Stephen, 1–11. Manchester: Manchester University Press.

Crocker, C., F. Osler Hampson, and P. Aall, eds. 2001. *Turbulent peace: The challenges of managing international conflict.* Washington, DC: United States Institute of Peace Press.

Cunningham, C., and S. Byrne. 2006. Peacebuilding in Belfast: Urban governance in polarized societies. *International Journal of World Peace* 23(1): 39–71.

Cunningham, M. J. 1991. *British government policy in Northern Ireland, 1969–89.* Manchester: Manchester University Press.

———. 1994. *British government and the Northern Ireland question: Governing a divided community.* Sheffield: PAVIC.

Curle, A. 1990. *Tools for transformation: A personal study.* Wallbridge: Hawthorn Press.

Darby, J. 1976. *Conflict in Northern Ireland: The development of a polarized community.* Dublin: Gill and Macmillan.

———. 2001. *The effects of violence on peace processes.* Washington, DC: United States Institute of Peace Press.

Darby, J., and R. MacGinty, eds. 2000. *The management of peace processes.* London: Palgrave Macmillan.

Denzin, N. 1989. *Interpretive biography.* New York: McGraw-Hill.

de Zeeuw, J., and K. Kumar, eds. 2006. *Promoting democracy in postconflict societies.* Boulder, CO: Lynne Rienner.

Diamond, L., and J. McDonald. 1996. *Multi-track diplomacy: A systems approach to peace.* West Hartford, CT: Kumarian Press.

Dixon, P. 1997. Paths to peace in Northern Ireland (I): Civil society and consociational approaches. *Democratization* 4(2): 1–27.

———. 2000. *Northern Ireland: Power, ideology and reality.* London: Macmillan.

———. 2007. *The Northern Ireland peace process: Choregraphy and theatrical politics.* London: Routledge.

Dos Santos, T. 1970. The structure of dependence. *American Economic Review* 60(2): 231–36.

Dowds, L., B. Hayes, and I. McAllister. 2005. The erosion of consent: Protestant disillusionment with the 1998 Good Friday Agreement. *Journal of Elections, Public Opinion and Parties* 15(1): 147–67.

Druckman, D. 2005. *Doing research: Methods of inquiry for conflict analysis.* Thousand Oaks, CA: Sage.

Dukes, F. 1996. *Resolving public conflict: Transforming community and governance.* Manchester: Manchester University Press.

Elliott, M. 2000. *The Catholics of Ulster: A history.* London: Allen Lane.

English, R. 2004. Sectarianism and politics in modern Ireland. In *Nothing but trouble: Religion and the Irish question*, edited by D. Kennedy, 26–50. Belfast: Irish Association for Cultural, Economic and Social Relations.

Escobar, A. 1994. *Encountering development: The making and unmaking of the third world*. Princeton: Princeton University Press.

Esman, M. 1991. Economic performance and ethnic conflict. In *Conflict and peacemaking in multiethnic societies*, edited by Joe V. Montville, 125–46. New York: Lexington Books.

———. 1994. *Ethnic politics*. Ithaca: Cornell University Press.

———. 1995. *International organizations and ethnic conflict*. Ithaca: Cornell University Press.

———. 1997. *Peaceworks: Can foreign aid moderate ethnic conflict?* Washington, DC: United States Institute of Peace Press.

European Union Court of Auditors. 2000. Special report No. 7 concerning the International Fund for Ireland and the Special Support Program for Peace and Reconciliation in Northern Ireland and the Border Counties of Ireland 1995 to 1999, together with the Commission's replies. Brussels: European Union Court of Auditors.

European Union Structural Funds. 1999. European Union Special Support Program for Peace and Reconciliation in Northern Ireland and the Border Counties of Ireland, 1995–1999. Brussels: European Structural Funds.

Farrell, M. 1980. *Northern Ireland: The orange state*. London: Pluto Press.

———. 1983. *Arming the Protestants*. London: Pluto Press.

Fisher, R. 1996. *Interactive conflict resolution*. Syracuse, NY: Syracuse University Press.

———. ed. 2005. *Paving the way: Contributions of interactive conflict resolution to peacemaking*. Lanham, MD: Lexington Books.

Fitzduff, M. 1996. *Beyond violence: Conflict resolution processes in Northern Ireland*. Tokyo: United Nations University.

Forman S., and S. Patrick. 2000. *Good intentions: Pledges of aid for postconflict recovery*. Boulder, CO: Lynne Rienner.

Freire, P. 1999. *Pedagogy of the oppressed*. New York: Continuum.

Friedman, J., and N. Killick. 1999. The partnering model. In *European centre for conflict prevention (ECCP): People building peace; 35 inspiring stories from around the world*. ECCP: Utrecht. Cited in Sandra Buchanan. 2005. Cost of conflict, price of peace: Conflict transformation through social and economic development. PhD dissertation, University of Ulster-Coleraine.

Gaffikin, F., and M. Morrisey. 1990. *Northern Ireland: The Thatcher years*. Atlantic Highlands, NJ: Zed Press.

Galtung, J. 1990. Cultural violence. *Journal of Peace Research* 27(3): 291–305.

———. 1996. *Peace by peaceful means: Peace and conflict, development and civilization*. Thousand Oaks, CA: Sage.

Goodhand, J. 2006. *Aiding peace? The role of NGOs in armed conflict*. Boulder, CO: Lynne Rienner.

———, and P. Atkinson. 2001. *Conflict and aid: Enhancing the peacebuilding impact of international engagement*. London: International Alert.

Grant, R., and J. Nijman, eds. 1998. *Global crisis in foreign aid–the foreign aid regime in flux: Crisis or tradition?* Syracuse, NY: Syracuse University Press.

Guelke, A. 1988. *Northern Ireland: The international perspective*. Dublin: Macmillan.

————. 2000. International dimensions of the Belfast agreement. In *Aspects of the Belfast Agreement,* edited by R. Wilford, 200–12. Oxford: Oxford University Press.

————. 2004. Religion, national identity and the conflict in Northern Ireland. In *The secular and the sacred: Nation, religion and politics,* edited by W. Safran, 101–21. Portland, OR: Frank Cass.

Gunder Frank, A. 1971. *Capitalism and underdevelopment in Latin America.* London: Penguin Books.

Gurr, T. R. 2000. *Peoples versus states: Minorities at risk in the new century.* Washington, DC: United States Institute of Peace Press.

Gurtov, M. 2007. *Global politics in the human interest.* Boulder, CO: Lynne Rienner.

Hampson, F. O. 1996. *Nurturing Peace: Why peace settlements succeed or fail.* Washington, DC: United States Institute of Peace Press.

Harris, R. 1972. *Prejudice and tolerance in Ulster: A study of neighbours and strangers in a border community.* Manchester: Manchester University Press.

Harvey, B. 1997. *Report on the program for peace and reconciliation.* York: Joseph Rowntree Charitable Trust.

————. 2003. *Review of the peace II program.* York: Joseph Rowntree Charitable Trust.

Hauss, C. 2001. *International conflict resolution: International relations for the 21st century.* New York: Continuum.

Hechter, M. 1975. *Internal colonialism: The Celtic fringe in British national development, 1536–1966.* London: Routledge and Kegan Paul.

Hevesi, A. G. 1994. *The MacBride principles and fair employment practices in Northern Ireland: A status report.* New York: Office of the Comptroller.

Hoy, P. 1998. *Players and issues in international aid.* West Hartford, CT: Kumarian Press.

International Fund for Ireland. 2004. Annual Report and Accounts. Dublin: IFI.

Irani, G., and N. Funk. 2001. Rituals of reconciliation: Arab-Islamic perspectives. In *Peace and conflict resolution in Islam: Precept and practice,* edited by A. A. Said, N. Funk, and A. S. Kadayifci, 1–25. Lanham, MD: University Press of America.

Irvin, C. 1999. *Militant nationalism: Between movement and party in Northern Ireland and the Basque country.* Duluth: University of Minnesota Press.

Irvin, C., and S. Byrne. 2002. The perception of economic aid in Northern Ireland and its role in the peace process. In *Change in Northern Ireland? The impact of the Good Friday agreement on politics and society,* edited by J. Neuheiser and S. Wolff, 167–91. Oxford: Berghahn Books.

Jeong, H. W. 2000. *Peace and conflict studies: An introduction.* Aldershot: Ashgate.

————. 2005. *Peacebuilding in postconflict Societies: Strategy and process.* Boulder, CO: Lynne Rienner.

Junne, G., and W. Verkoren, eds. 2004. *Post conflict development: Meeting new challenges.* Boulder, CO: Lynne Rienner

Kaufman, S. 2001. *Modern hatreds: The symbolic politics of ethnic war.* Ithaca: Cornell University Press.

Keashly, L., and R. J. Fisher. 1996. A contingency perspective on conflict interventions: Theoretical and practical considerations. In *Resolving international conflicts: The theory and practice of mediation,* edited by J. Bercovitch, 235–63. Boulder, CO: Lynne Rienner.

Kelman, H. 1997. Group processes in the resolution of international conflicts: Experiences from the Israeli-Palestinian case. *American Psychologist* 52: 212–20.

Knox, C., and P. Quirk. 2000. *Peace building in Northern Ireland, Israel and South Africa: Transition, transformation and reconciliation.* New York: St. Martin's Press.

Kosic, A., and I. Favretto. 2007. *Promoting reconciliation through youth: Inter-ethnic community mobilization.* PRAYIC project. Research funded by the European Commission through the Marie Curie Intra-European Fellowship, 1–38.

KPMG Management Consulting. 1995. *The International Fund for Ireland: Assessment of the fund's impacts on contact, dialogue and reconciliation between the communities and on employment.* Dublin.

———. 2001. *The International Fund for Ireland: Assessment of the fund's impact on contact, dialogue and reconciliation between the communities and on employment.* Dublin.

Kriesberg, L. 1998. *Constructive conflicts: From escalation to resolution.* Lanham, MD: Rowman and Littlefield.

———. 2002. Coexistence and reconciliation of communal conflicts. In *The handbook of interethnic coexistence*, edited by E. Weiner, 182–98. New York: Continuum.

Leahy, P. 1995. *Senator Patrick: Congressional record.* (February 22) p. s2917. Cited in C. Irvin and S. Byrne. 2002. The perception of economic aid in Northern Ireland and its role in the peace process. In *Change in Northern Ireland? The impact of the Good Friday agreement on politics and society,* edited by J. Neuheiser and S. Wolff, 134. Oxford: Berghahn Books.

Lederach, J. P. 1995. *Preparing for peace: Conflict transformation across cultures.* Syracuse, NY: Syracuse University Press.

———. 1997. *Building peace: Sustainable reconciliation in divided societies,* Washington, DC: United States Institute of Peace.

———. 1999a. *The journey toward reconciliation.* Scottsdale, PA: Herald.

———. 1999b. Justpeace: The challenge of the 21st century. In *People building peace.* Sweden: European Centre for Conflict Prevention.

———. 2002. Beyond violence: Building sustainable peace. In *The Handbook of interethnic coexistence*, edited by E. Weiner, 236–45. New York: Continuum.

———. 2005. *The moral imagination: The art and soul of building peace.* Oxford: Oxford University Press.

Licklider, R. 2001. Obstacles to peace settlements. In *Turbulent peace: The challenges of managing international conflict,* edited by C. Crocker, F. Osler Hampson, and P. Aall, 697–718. Washington, DC: United States Institute of Peace Press.

Lijphart, A. 1977. *Democracy in plural societies: A comparative exploration.* New Haven: Yale University Press.

Love, M. T. 1995. *Peace building through reconciliation in Northern Ireland.* Aldershot: Avebury.

Lyons, T. 2005. *Demilitarizing politics: Elections on the uncertain road to peace.* Boulder, CO: Lynne Rienner.

Mason, D., and J. Meernik, eds. 2005. *Conflict prevention and peacebuilding in post war societies.* Abingdon, Oxford: Routledge.

McCann, E. 1974. *War and an Irish town.* Harmondsworth: Penguin.

McGarry, J. 1998. Political settlements in Northern Ireland and South Africa. *Political Studies* 46(5): 1–17.

———. 2001. *Northern Ireland and the divided world: The Northern Ireland conflict and the Good Friday Agreement in comparative perspective.* Oxford: Oxford University Press.

McGarry, J., and B. O'Leary. 1995. *Explaining Northern Ireland: Broken images.* Cambridge, MA: Blackwell.

————. 2004. *The Northern Ireland conflict: Consociational engagements.* Oxford: Oxford University Press.

————. 2007. *Politics of antagonism: Understanding Northern Ireland.* Abingdon, Oxford: Routledge.

Memmi, A. 1974. *The colonizer and the colonized.* London: Souvenir Press.

Miall, H., O. Ramsbotham, and T. Woodhouse. 1999. *Contemporary conflict resolution: The prevention, management and transformation of deadly conflicts.* Cambridge: Polity Press.

Minow, M. 1998. *Between vengeance and forgiveness.* Boston, MA: Beacon Press.

Mitchel, P. 2003. *Evangelicalism and national identity in Ulster, 1921–1998.* Oxford: Oxford University Press.

Mitchell, C. 2006. *Religion, identity and politics in Northern Ireland.* Aldershot: Ashgate.

Morgan, A., and B. Purdie, eds. 1980. *Ireland: Divided nation, divided class.* London: Ink Links.

Munck, R. 1985. *Ireland: Nation, State and Class Struggle.* London: Westview Press.

O'Dowd, L., B. Rolston, and M. Tomlinson. 1980. *Northern Ireland: Between civil rights and civil wars.* London: CSE Books.

O'Leary, B., and J. McGarry. 1993. *The politics of antagonism: Understanding Northern Ireland.* Atlantic Highlands, NJ: Athlone.

OECD. 1999. Geographical distribution of financial flows to aid recipients.

Paisley, I., J. Hume, and J. Nicholson. 1997. Special support program for peace and reconciliation in Northern Ireland and the border counties of Ireland revisited. Report to Jacques Santer, president of the European Commission. Belfast.

Paffenholz, T. 2000. *Community cased bottom up peacebuilding.* Uppsala, Sweden: Life and Peace Institute.

————. 2005. Challenge 1: The need to renew the policy challenge after ten years of linking peacebuilding to development. Forty-eighth Annual International Studies Association Convention, Honolulu, Hawaii.

Paffenholz, T., and L. Reychler. 2005. Challenge 2. Assessing the role of aid in peacebuilding: From single tools towards a holistic peace and conflict intervention assessment systems (PCIAS). Forty-eighth Annual International Studies Association Convention, Honolulu, Hawaii.

Pearson, F. 2001. Dimensions of conflict resolution in ethnopolitical disputes. *Journal of Peace Research* 38(3): 275–88.

Peck, C. 1998. *Sustainable peace: The role of the UN and regional organizations in preventing conflict.* Lanham, MD: Rowman and Littlefield.

Peshkin, A. 1993. The goodness of qualitative research. *Educational Researcher* 22(2): 1–28.

Pollak, A. 1993. *A citizen's inquiry: The Opsahl report of Northern Ireland.* Dublin: Lilliput Press.

PricewaterhouseCoopers. 2003. Special EU programs body. Ex-post evaluation of Peace I, and mid-term evaluation of Peace II final report. Belfast.

Princen, T. 1991. *Intermediaries in international conflicts.* Princeton: Princeton University Press.

Probert, B. 1978. *Beyond orange and green: The political economy of the Northern Ireland crisis.* London: Zed Books.

Pugh, M., and J. Goodhand. 2005. *War economies in a regional context: Challenges of transformation.* Boulder, CO: Lynne Rienner.

Redekop, V. N. 2002. *From violence to blessing: How an understanding of deep-rooted conflict can open paths to reconciliation.* Toronto, ON: Novalis.

Reychler, L., and T. Paffenholz, eds. 2001. *Peacebuilding: A field guide.* Boulder, CO: Lynne Rienner.

Rigby, A. 2001. *Justice and reconciliation: After the violence.* Boulder, CO: Lynne Rienner.

Rolston, B., and M. Tomlinson. 1988. *Unemployment in West Belfast: The Obair report.* Belfast: Beyond the Pale Publications.

Rose, R. 1971. *Governing without consensus: An Irish perspective.* London: Faber and Faber.

Ross, M. H. 1993. *The management of conflicts: Interpretations and interests in comparative perspectives.* New Haven, CT: Yale University Press.

Rothman, J. 1997. *Resolving identity based conflicts.* San Francisco, CA: Jossey Bass.

Rowthorn, B., and N. Wayne. 1988. *Northern Ireland: The political economy of conflict.* Cambridge: Polity Press.

Ryan, S. 1996. Peacebuilding strategies and intercommunal conflict: Approaches to the transformation of divided societies. *Nationalism and Ethnic Conflicts* 2(2): 216–31.

———. 2007. *The transformation of violent intercommunal conflict.* Aldershot: Ashgate.

Sandole, D. 1999. *Capturing the complexity of conflict: Dealing with violent ethnic conflicts in the post cold war era.* New York: Pinter.

———. 2002. Virulent ethnocentrism: A major challenge for transformational conflict resolution and peacebuilding in the post-cold war era. *Global Review of Ethnopolitics* 1(2): 4–27.

———. 2006. Traditional "realism" versus the "new" realism: John W. Burton, conflict prevention and the elusive "paradigm shift." *Global Society* 20(4): 543–62.

Schirch, L. 2004. *Ritual and symbol in peacebuilding.* West Hartford, CT: Kumarian Press.

Schwerin, E. W. 1995. *Mediation, citizen empowerment, and transformational politics.* Westport, CT: Greenwood.

Scott, J. 1998. *Seeing like a state: How certain schemes to improve the human condition have failed.* New Haven, CT: Yale University Press.

Senehi, J. 1996. Language, culture and conflict: Storytelling as a matter of life and death. *Mind and Human Interaction* 7(3): 150–64.

———. 2000. Constructive storytelling in inter-communal conflicts: Building community, building peace. In *Reconcilable differences: Turning points in ethnopolitical conflict,* edited by S. Byrne and C. Irvin, 96–115. West Hartford, CT: Kumarian.

———. 2002. Constructive storytelling: A peace process. *Peace and Conflict Studies* 9(2): 41–63.

Senehi, J., and S. Byrne. 2006. From violence toward peace: The role of storytelling for youth healing and political empowerment after social conflict. In *Troublemakers or peacemakers: Youth and post-accord peace building,* edited by S. McEvoy, 235–58. South Bend, IN: University of Notre Dame Press.

Smith, A. D. 2003. *Chosen peoples: Sacred sources of national identity.* Oxford: Oxford University Press.

Smith, J. A. 1995. Semi-structured interviewing and qualitative analysis. In *Rethinking methods in psychology,* edited by J. A. Smith, R. Harré, and L. Van Langenhove, 30–57. London: Sage.

Snyder, A. 2005. *Women and development.* London: Ashgate.

Teague, P., ed. 1987. *Beyond the rhetoric: Politics, the economy and social policy in Northern Ireland.* London: Lawrence and Wishart.

Tomlinson, M. 1995. The British economic subvention and the Irish peace process. *International Policy Review* 5(1): 20–35.

Tschirgi, N. 2003. *Peacebuilding as the link between security and development: Is the window of opportunity closing?* New York: International Peace Academy Studies in Security and Development.

Tuso, H. 2000. Indigenous processes of conflict resolution in Oromo society. In *Traditional cures for modern African conflicts: African conflict medicine*, edited by W. I. Zartman, 79–94. Boulder, CO: Lynne Rienner.

Tutu, D. 1999. *No future without forgiveness.* New York: Doubleday.

Ury, W. L., J. M. Brett, and S. B. Goldberg. 1993. *Getting disputes resolved: Designing systems to cut the costs of conflict.* Harvard, MA: PON Books.

Van Tongeren, P., M. Hellema, and J. Verhoeven, eds. 2005. *People peacebuilding II: Successful stories of civil society.* Boulder, CO: Lynne Rienner.

Varynen, R. 1997. Economic incentives and the Bosnian peace process. In *The price of peace: Incentives and international conflict prevention*, edited by David Cortright, 155–80. Boulder, CO: Rowman and Littlefield.

Volkan, V. 1998. *Blood lines: From ethnic pride to ethnic terrorism.* Boulder, CO: Westview Press.

Wallerstein, I. 1988. *The modern world–System III.* San Diego: Academic Press.

———. 2004. *World systems analysis: An introduction.* Raleigh, NC: Duke University Press.

Webel, C., and J. Galtung, eds. 2007. *Handbook of peace and conflict studies.* Abingdon, Oxford: Routledge.

Wenger, A., and D. Mockli. 2005. *Conflict prevention: The untapped potential of the business sector.* Boulder, CO: Lynne Rienner.

White House Conference for Trade and Investment in Ireland, Northern Ireland, and the Border Counties of Ireland (May 24–26, 1995). Washington, DC: White House.

Whyte, J. 1990. *Interpreting Northern Ireland: An appraisal.* Oxford: Clarendon Press.

Wood, B. 2001. Development dimensions of conflict prevention and peacebuilding. An Independent Study prepared for the Bureau for Crisis Prevention and Recovery. Ottawa, ON: UNDP.

Woodward, S. L. 2005. Economic priorities for successful peace implementation. In *Ending civil wars: Implementation of peace agreements*, edited by S. J. Stedman, D. Rothchild, and E. M. Cousens, 183–214. Boulder, CO: Lynne Rienner.

Woolpert, S., C. D. Slaton, and E. W. Schwerin, eds. 1998. *Transformational politics: Theory, study and practice.* Albany, NY: SUNY Press.

Wright, F. 1973. Protestant ideology and politics in Ulster. *European Journal of Sociology* 15: 213–80.

———. 1987. *Northern Ireland: A comparative analysis.* Dublin: Gill and Macmillan.

———. 1996. *Two lands on one soil: Ulster politics before home rule.* London: Palgrave Macmillan.

Index